# MYTHIC VISION
## *The Making of*

# eragon

## MARK COTTA VAZ

**DOUBLEDAY**

To Christopher Paolini and the Paolini family, who dreamed a grand dream and made it come true.

—M.C.V.

MYTHIC VISION
A DOUBLEDAY BOOK 978 0 385 61159 6 (from January 2007)
0 385 61159 5

Published in Great Britain by Doubleday, an imprint of Random House Children's Books

This edition published 2006

1 3 5 7 9 10 8 6 4 2



Eragon photography by David Appleby, Juliana Malucelli, James Dittiger, and Frank Ockenfels





...NDOM HOUSE CHILDREN'S BOOKS
...53 Uxbridge Road, London W5 5SA
...ion of The Random House Group Ltd

...NDOM HOUSE AUSTRALIA (PTY) LTD
...lfred Street, Milsons Point, Sydney,
...ew South Wales 2061, Australia

...NDOM HOUSE NEW ZEALAND LTD
...oad, Glenfield, Auckland 10, New Zealand

RANDOM HOUSE (PTY) LTD
...n, Corner Boundary Road & Carse O'Gowrie,
Houghton 2198, South Africa

...RANDOM HOUSE INDIA PVT LTD
301 World Trade Tower, Hotel Intercontinental Grand Complex,
Barakhamba Lane, New Delhi 110001, India

THE RANDOM HOUSE GROUP Limited Reg. No. 954009
www.kidsatrandomhouse.co.uk

A CIP catalogue record for this book is available from the British Library.

Printed and bound in Italy

# CONTENTS

CHAPTER ONE: The Dreaming                          8

CHAPTER TWO: Journey Story                        24

CHAPTER THREE: Casting Call                       36

CHAPTER FOUR: The Land of Alagaësia               52

CHAPTER FIVE: Legends of *Eragon*                 74

CHAPTER SIX: The Dragon's Realm                   90

CHAPTER SEVEN: The Battle of Farthen Dûr         112

CHAPTER EIGHT: "That's How Legends Go"           130

"The sands of time cannot be stopped. Years pass whether we will them or not . . . but we can remember. What has been lost may yet live on in memories. That which you will hear is imperfect and fragmented, yet treasure it, for without you it does not exist. I give you now a memory that has been forgotten, hidden in the dreamy haze that lies behind us."

—*Brom, the storyteller, from* Eragon, *Book One of the Inheritance trilogy*

# CHAPTER ONE

# the Dreaming

*O*n a cold, moonlit night, the icy wind that howled through the forest carried with it "a scent that would change the world." That scent meant prey to the sorcerer Durza: the scent of three elves on horseback. Two were armed escorts for Arya, who carried a heavy pouch that held what looked like a gleaming sapphire stone. Durza was waiting in ambush with twelve monstrous Urgals. He attacked, killing the escorts and capturing Arya—but not before she uttered a mystical incantation and, in a flash of emerald light, teleported her precious stone far away. The blue stone appeared in the forested mountain range known as the Spine, exploding near where a fifteen-year-old boy named Eragon was hunting. Eragon had no fresh meat to show for his labor, but the next morning he would rise with the sun for the long walk home, taking with him the strange blue stone. . . .

Thus the scene was set for *Eragon,* a fantasy novel that was a publishing phenomenon when Twentieth Century Fox purchased the film rights. The turnaround from book to big screen was swift—*Eragon,* published in 2003 by Alfred A. Knopf Books for Young Readers of Random House Children's Books, was ushered into theaters by the Christmas season of 2006. The characters in the book would take on the flesh-and-blood form of stellar actors, mythical locations would be duplicated in dramatic sets and rugged locations, and one of the book's most fantastical aspects—a flying dragon —would be realized with all the wizardry of the most storied visual effects house in movie history.

Eragon's first encounter with the newly hatched dragon.

## THE NEXT GREAT FANTASY

At the beginning of the production, the behind-the-scenes word was that Fox felt it had another potential *Star Wars* franchise. The movie was still in production when advance studio publicity hailed *Eragon* as "The Next Great Fantasy." As all great fantasies do, the story conjured another world, in this case the land of Alagaësia, a kingdom stretching from the western coastal wilderness of the Spine into the inland Hadarac Desert, which spread to the southern summits of the Beor Mountains. It was a world of humans, sorcerers, monsters, elves, and dwarves—even mighty dragons were not so much the stuff of legend as a lingering memory.

But Alagaësia was not a happy kingdom—over all loomed the shadow of King Galbatorix. The brutal ruler could summon the dark magic of Durza, who was a powerful Shade (a sorcerer possessed by evil spirits), and the demonic mercenaries known as the Ra'zac, while an army of Urgals stood ready to enforce his iron will. The remote village of

Carvahall, nestled in the Spine's northern Palancar Valley, had long resisted the king, thanks to its primordial, impenetrable forests, but even Palancar lay in the shadow of fear.

It would be to Eragon's eventual sorrow that fate entrusted him with the mission of saving Alagaësia from the stranglehold of Galbatorix. But his adventure began with wonder, as he soon discovered it was not a shiny blue stone he had brought home from his hunting expedition in the Spine—it was a dragon egg. From the sapphire shell hatched a blue-hued female of a species believed to have been driven to extinction (except for King Galbatorix's own dragon). Eragon named the dragon Saphira, and from the beginning, boy and dragon were kindred spirits. Their bond would grow through an arduous journey beyond the borders of any place or experience Eragon had ever known.

The courier elf Arya, bearing that rarest of wonders—a dragon egg—is met on the lonely forest path by the Shade Durza.

In a desperate attempt to save the precious dragon egg, Arya teleports it moments before she is captured by Durza.

Christopher Paolini, the author of *Eragon,* has joked that his own life seemed to parallel Eragon's journey (minus flying dragons, of course). Like his main character, he left the familiar comforts of home, although in Paolini's case it wasn't a quest to save a kingdom, but in service of book tours through the United States and Europe. But like that of his fictional alter ego, Paolini's life and work seemed touched with magic. He wrote *Eragon* because he didn't have the vast sums of money to make a movie

The glorious sight of the Beartooth Mountains.

of the epic story in his head—it was beyond his wildest dreams that within a few years a major Hollywood studio would do exactly that.

There were many creative inspirations for the mythic tale, but at its heart, *Eragon* reflected Paolini's personal experiences, his Tom Sawyer boyhood growing up in a valley of the Beartooth Mountains of Montana, a place not unlike the Palancar Valley that Eragon called home.

## MONTANA INSPIRATIONS FOR *ERAGON*

The Beartooth Mountains are thousands of square miles of wilderness and home to grizzly bears, elk, bison, mountain goats, and deer. Legends abound in these soaring peaks. One tale from frontier days tells of a pack of gray wolves who prowled the night for human babies, killing males but carrying off females to raise as their own cubs. A ranching family in the Beartooth lost their baby girl to the wolves, and for years thereafter, cowboys, prospectors, and Indians coming out of the mountains reported glimpses of a wolf pack and the naked white girl with long brown hair who ran with them. The she-wolf, now a young woman, was finally captured, thanks to a Sioux Indian with the magic gift of finding lost things. The woman was weaned from her wolfish ways and her happy parents even saw her wedding day. But the wedding night was interrupted by the growl of wolves outside the house. Despite his bride's pleas not to leave her alone, the bridegroom went to investigate. When he returned, their bedroom was empty, his bride's wedding gown fallen on the floor and the night wind blowing through the open window. The woman was never seen by human eyes again.

Such are the strange tales that come out of a wilderness forged from ancient ice and molten fire. Volcanic explosions once covered the western and central peaks of the Beartooth, and the range has some of the most soaring elevations in the lower forty-eight states, including the highest point in Big Sky country—Granite Peak, which rises to 12,799 feet.

Christopher Paolini grew up in a valley of the Beartooth Mountains with his parents, Kenneth and Talita, and his sister, Angela. There is a rainy side to the valley, but they make their home on the dry side, among the juniper trees, scrub, grass, and rattlesnakes. Because of the valley's shape, television reception wasn't possible until three or four years ago, so the family lived without broadcast television ("a great way of growing up," Paolini adds). What the Paolini family did get, every time they looked out a window, was the glorious sight of the Beartooth Mountains.

The film would create its own vision of Alagaësia.

Christopher Paolini at home in Montana.

"I grew up hiking and camping in those mountains and playing alongside the Yellowstone River," Paolini recalled. "I made my own bows and arrows. In the mountains I've found fossils of small creatures. Once, I found a hand-cast musket ball buried inside the trunk of a tree, which someone must have been using for target practice. The weather is notoriously extreme in Montana and I've been caught in a couple thunderstorms up in the mountains, which is dangerous because if you get soaked you run the risk of hypothermia. Two years ago, I was hiking with my great-uncle Bruce and my sister, and suddenly we ran into a brown bear, which gets the heart going quite a bit. The bear sort of looked at us and then turned tail, but that's when you realize you're not at the top of the food chain anymore. All these experiences played into my love of nature and the outdoors. The land of Alagaësia is largely based on where I live along the Beartooth Mountains and the Yellowstone River."

Paolini's personal experience of the glacial cold of the mountains, the excitement of encountering wildlife, being in the face of howling winds and thunderstorms—all that and more enriched *Eragon*. If one unfurled a map of Alagaësia (a map,

The Beartooth Mountains, which inspired Paolini's vision of the Beor Mountains.

incidentally, that Paolini himself drew for his book), a correlation could be drawn between the fanciful geography and real landmarks of the place Paolini calls home. The Spine is a place of "misfortune and bad luck," where Eragon has hiked for years, wary of its dangers but open to its secrets—much like the author's own experiences in the Beartooth. The sparsely populated Palancar Valley and the village of Carvahall were inspired by the rimmed valley where the Paolini family lives. The Beartooth also influenced Paolini's creation of the ten-mile-high Beor Mountains—"I just took the mountains I love so much and paid them tribute by making them ten times bigger." (There's even a Beartooth River in the Beor Mountains.)

Other pieces of *Eragon* geography were inspired by landmarks visited on various travels. A trip to the Carlsbad Caverns inspired Paolini's creation of Farthen Dûr, a fortress city of dwarves inside a volcanic crater deep in the Beor Mountains, where the rebel forces known as the Varden take refuge from Galbatorix. "There's no better preparation for writing about dwarves than going down into the Carlsbad Caverns," Paolini said with a chuckle.

## THE WRITER'S JOURNEY

But the forging of *Eragon* was more than the sum of places and personal experiences. Integral to the saga's creation was the close-knit Paolini family and their support of Christopher's literary ambitions. The family always encouraged a love of education, and Talita Paolini, a Montessori-trained teacher, homeschooled Christopher and Angela. That self-discipline was vital for a budding writer. Christopher began research and preparations for the book in the fall of 1998, when he was fourteen years old, and at fifteen, the same age as the saga's hero, he began writing in earnest.

"My initial inspiration was the idea of a boy who finds a dragon egg that hatches, and the boy and his dragon go on a series of adventures. I had previously tried writing stories, but they always flatlined after about five or six pages. So before I started *Eragon*, I spent a couple months reading as many books as I could on writing, on constructing plots and creating characters. I also did a fair amount of research, almost as if I were doing an historical novel. I read a lot of Norse and Icelandic mythology, *Beowulf* and things like that. I was trying to create a pseudo-European world, but with its own history and internal logic."

Paolini spent a month plotting not just one book-length tale, but a trilogy he christened *Inheritance*. (His efforts included inventing different languages for his imaginary world.) Only after he decided what would happen in each book did he begin writing book one: *Eragon*. The typical workday began each morning with Christopher closing his door and sitting at his computer for "solid bursts" of writing that would be interrupted only for lunch and an hour of exercise before dinner. He zealously guarded the work, not sharing a page with his parents or sister, who became increasingly curious about what was being fed into Christopher's word processor as the weeks and months went by.

With words he built a world, and some of his imaginings were spectacular sights he always wished to have seen in a movie. One such set piece was the hollow volcanic cone of Farthen Dûr, which was ten miles high and wide and held the mile-high white marble city of Tronjheim, its ceiling topped by a gigantic red star sapphire sixty feet across and carved into the shape of a rose.

Another fantasy was to dream up the most unusual dragon ever, and from his imagination sprang Saphira, who was not only female but had blue scales set like faceted, gleaming gems. "I used blue for Saphira because I'm partially color-blind and I see more blue in the world than most people. An optometrist said I even see shades of purple as blue. Blue and purple are the colors of royalty, and Saphira is nothing if not regal. Eragon has a special relationship with Saphira—they would die for each other. I was trying to make Saphira the best friend anyone could have, and I thought, it would be nice to have a brilliant, sapphire blue dragon who could eat anyone you didn't like and who you could fly around on."

A year after he began, Christopher finished book one of his *Inheritance* trilogy and he finally had something to show for his efforts. "It was terrible, awful," he recalled. "The story was there but the writing needed work. I spent another year and rewrote the book, fleshing out the characters and dialogue. And at the end of the second year, I handed the manuscript to my parents. I hadn't shown it to them until I had the second draft. All they knew was I was working on a book about a young boy and a dragon. So they were very curious and probably a bit concerned about how I was spending my time, locked away in my room and working on this thing."

His parents loved the manuscript. Then came the fateful family meeting in which Christopher was asked how far he wanted to take his writing project. His parents had experience in self-publishing, including ten years his father had spent in graphic design and as a "pre-press" person in the pre-computer days, when typeset copy was laid out by hand. Instead of the manuscript getting lost in the maze of big-time publishers, was Christopher interested in having his story self-published? The answer was yes, and *Eragon* became the Paolini family business.

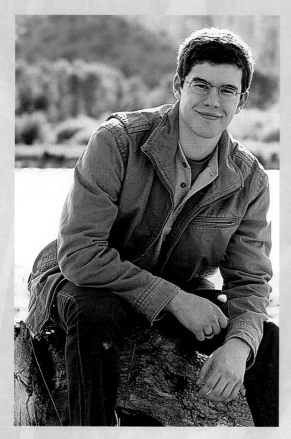

"I'm all the characters [not just Eragon], even the bad ones. It is fun—it allows you to get inside someone else's head and depict people acting in ways you wouldn't normally act. When I'm doing my job properly, I feel the characters are speaking for themselves. I'm not trying to tell the characters what to say, but *listening* to what they are trying to say. When I used to hear authors say stuff like that, I would think they were slightly bonkers. But I've come to understand that point of view."

—Christopher Paolini

# THE PAOLINI FAMILY ADVENTURE

In the process of self-publishing *Eragon*, the Paolini family performed the functions undertaken by entire departments at publishing houses: editing, typesetting, proofreading, design and layout, production, marketing, storage, and distribution. It took a year for the family to create the final book, which they produced in an oversized paperback edition. As a finishing touch, Christopher provided original cover art depicting the mystical eye of the dragon. "When you work on a thing for three years, that thing becomes you," Paolini mused. "So when we got the first proof copy of *Eragon*, it was an incredible experience, almost like seeing your own baby. . . . I can't even put it into words."

But years removed from his seminal work, Paolini reflects that it's too "painful" to reread *Eragon*. His comment was partly the normal self-awareness of a young writer who, with experience, could look back on a first work and think only of how he would do things differently. But his first book was also a reminder of how tough the project had been for his family. "There were financial pressures after we decided to make *Eragon* the family business. My parents weren't getting any other income during the year it took to get ready for publication. So it was produced under a lot of stress. By the time we started trying to sell *Eragon*, if it had taken a few more months to turn a profit, we were going to have to sell the house. It was do or die."

The family had begun selling the book through bookstore appearances, but that was a slow, uncertain process. It was a major excursion just getting to the bookstores sprinkled across Montana's wide-open spaces, and hit-or-miss trying to interest whoever might appear. Christopher did his best to get the attention of potential customers. Given his novel's quasi-medieval atmosphere, he dressed the part, with a billowy red swordsman's shirt, black pantaloons, a black pirate belt, and black knee-high, lace-up leather boots.

During a family meeting around the kitchen table, his mother suggested they could reach hundreds at a time through presentations at

**The Knopf edition of *Eragon*.**

schools and libraries. With his father at the wheel, *Eragon* forays crisscrossed not only Montana but Idaho, Texas, and Washington State—over 135 presentations, by Paolini's estimate.

Along the way, word spread and copies sold. Initial printings of fifty to a hundred became thousand-copy runs. The nomadic adventure was exhilarating, but also a tough go that crossed hundreds of miles of asphalt. Exhausting days ended in hotel rooms, where Christopher would fall asleep and find himself doing his spiel in his dreams: *"Hi, my name is Christopher Paolini. Do you like fantasy? Well, you should check out* Eragon. *It's the story of a young man and his dragon. . . ."*

But the self-publishing adventure was about to end.

In October 2002, the *Eragon* road show came to Island Books bookstore on Mercer Island, near Seattle. Christopher's mother had received an e-mail from New York and passed on the happy message that Michelle Frey, an editor at the Knopf imprint of Random House Children's Books, wanted to buy not only *Eragon* but the entire planned *Inheritance* trilogy. "We were sort of bouncing off the ceilings for a few hours," Paolini recalled. "But we were really puzzled, because we hadn't submitted the book to any publisher and we didn't know how they found out about it."

It turned out that bestselling author Carl Hiaasen had been on a fly-fishing vacation in Montana with his wife and twelve-year-old stepson, Ryan, who picked up a copy of *Eragon* at a local bookstore. He enjoyed it so much, Hiaasen recommended it to his editor at Knopf, Nancy Siscoe, who passed the book to Frey, who fell in love with it. Frey expressed her interest in buying the trilogy through an e-mail address the Paolinis had listed in the back of the book. "I read so many submissions," Frey explained, "but I couldn't put this book down. I was sucked into the world of Alagaësia and the lives of the characters. I felt that Christopher was an incredibly gifted storyteller who had a sense of epic, and I wanted to share that with others."

"I always like to tell young readers you can change the world," Paolini reflected. "A young reader certainly changed *my* world, and I'm forever in his debt. And, of course, Michelle basically said, 'Oh, I'll take a chance on an eighteen-year-old with a fantasy trilogy that's been self-published!' That took guts!"

**Ed Speleers, as Eragon, looks out over the sweeping vista of Alagaësia.**

Once *Eragon* was bought by Random House, it went through another editorial phase before being published in August 2003. *Eragon* debuted at number 3 on the *New York Times* bestseller list. It was an improbable success story, but there was more to come, including several strange coincidences. "John Jude Palencar is one of my favorite artists—I named Palancar Valley after him," Paolini noted. "But without knowing, and without them telling me, that's exactly who Knopf picked to paint the covers for the three books in the trilogy! That is *really* weird!"

## THE CALL OF HOLLYWOOD

Then came Christopher's triumphant return to the same Seattle-area bookstore where he had received the exciting offer from Knopf. "I was at [Island Books] when I got a call from my parents and my agent saying that Fox had expressed an interest in acquiring the film rights for *Eragon*. It looked like a good offer, and we agreed to it. It was quite a coincidence."

The studio's Fox 2000 division had purchased the rights, a deal made by Fox 2000 president Elizabeth Gabler and creative executive Rodney Ferrell. *Eragon* was then put on the Hollywood fast track to production. One of the early decisions was a seemingly risky one, as the studio decided to entrust the potential franchise to a first-time director, Industrial Light & Magic (ILM) visual effects supervisor Stefen Fangmeier.

"A big challenge in bringing the written word into the visual realm is that everybody who has read the book has their own imagination about things such as what the dragon looks like," said *Eragon* producer Wyck Godfrey. "But at the end of the day, this is a universal story about a boy who comes from nothing and eventually realizes he's the most pivotal character in the entire kingdom, which is a great wish fulfillment for kids growing up. Everyone wants to feel they're destined for something great. So you want to bring in a filmmaker who has a specific vision that can coincide with the vision of what is in the book. Stefen Fangmeier had that. He came in with a very strong vision of this world. It wasn't *Harry Potter*, it wasn't the *Lord of the Rings*. It was the world of *Eragon*."

# CHAPTER TWO

# Journey Story

A wide range of crafts and production departments fit into the big picture of moviemaking, but few aspects are as misunderstood as visual effects, where the very term "effects film" stands for an entire genre of blockbuster productions. It's a technology-driven craft, one in which the artistry and storytelling involved are often missed by critics or audiences overwhelmed by the final spectacle. Indeed, visual effects seem to be thought of as a modern branch of the hallowed tree that sprouted from the magical legend of Merlin. Of course, effects artists have always been expected to create miracles and have always tried to oblige. It's the art of illusions, made to order—welcome to Stefen Fangmeier's world.

Director Stefen Fangmeier gets ready to film in King Galbatorix's throne-room set while actors John Malkovich and Robert Carlyle chat in the background. Fangmeier, an accomplished visual effects supervisor at Industrial Light & Magic, made his directorial debut with *Eragon*. "I think what attracted people to the books is that Christopher did a great job in weaving together different fantasy elements, such as dwarves and elves and, of course, the relationship between Eragon and Saphira," Fangmeier noted. "Chris created a world that people could submerge themselves in, and that's what I hoped to be able to do with the film."

# THE DIRECTOR'S VISION

Before winning the directorial assignment for *Eragon,* Fangmeier had risen through the ranks to become one of the leading visual effects supervisors at Industrial Light & Magic, Lucasfilm's famed visual effects company. Fangmeier arrived on the scene at the dawn of the digital revolution, working on such breakthrough films as *Terminator 2* and *Jurassic Park.* Fangmeier's specialty included "invisible" effects, such as the nineteenth-century warships, naval battles, and raging seas he and co–visual effects supervisor Nathan McGuinness helped create for the seafaring epic *Master and Commander: The Far Side of the World.*

Time and again, Fangmeier had demonstrated his chops in handling cutting-edge technology, the artistic sensibility to create shots with mood and artful composition, and the narrative ability to move a story forward. In other words, he was an accomplished storyteller. But as a director, Fangmeier would have to focus on *everything* about making a movie, from finalizing a script and casting to overseeing production design and cinematography, working with the actors, editing, and approving the visual effects work. "The amount of information a director needs to divulge is huge," said *Eragon* first assistant director Chris Newman. "People will ask you everything, from how much sugar you want in your tea to what you want the music to do in a particular scene."

Fangmeier confers with Ed Speleers, who would credit the first-time director with providing both direction and the freedom for the actor to find Eragon within himself.

Fangmeier's involvement began in October 2004, when he received the first draft of the *Eragon* screenplay written by Peter Buchman. "It was a very good read and exciting to have this kind of script offered to me as a first-time director. Of course, I knew that with the fantasy aspect, people would look at me in terms of the visual effects requirements. I always expected that I would direct a film that had a lot of visual spectacle, and *Eragon* is a journey story, where a small world gets expanded and ends at this fantastic and exotic place inside a volcano. However, my first reaction to the script was it was a great story that had an emotional arc."

Fangmeier's initial challenge was to further develop the script and start bringing his own vision to the production. As with any adaptation of an existing work for the screen, the sprawling narrative of a novel covering hundreds of pages had to fit the structure of a motion picture with an approximately two-hour running time. (Paolini notes the movie was simply "a different beast" from the book.) For example, the relationship between Eragon and Saphira, which flowered and unfolded across the

Fangmeier helps Robert Carlyle get into a menacing mood.

Taking a break in the action at the Carvahall set in Hungary are (left to right) Chris Newman, Stefen Fangmeier, Hugh Johnson, and Jeremy Irons.

length of the book, had to be condensed for the film. In the book, a host of new characters and situations are introduced when Eragon and Saphira arrive at the Varden stronghold at Farthen Dûr, while in the movie the Varden refuge comes at the top of the third and last act, too late to expect audiences to accept too many new characters. Thus, events in the movie accelerate after Eragon arrives at Farthen Dûr, with a battle between the rebels and Galbatorix's invading forces coming sooner than in the book. Some of the characters Eragon encounters later in his journey in the book made it into the movie, including the young swordsman Murtagh and Ajihad, a Varden general. But other characters, notably the dwarf Orik, didn't make the cut. In Orik's case, the storytelling situations he served in the book were transferred to the already introduced character of Murtagh. (Producer Wyck Godfrey notes that Orik is planned to be introduced early in the projected sequel.)

As the script was honed, other major decisions went forward. It was clear Saphira would be computer-generated—an assignment that went to Fangmeier's old employer, ILM, based in San Francisco. But other than a digital dragon, the production possibilities were wide-open. In recent years, productions have had actors perform on stages filled with bluescreen or greenscreen, the neutral backing that allows the footage of actors and props to be combined with background imagery a filmmaker scans into the computer for a digital composite shot. Films such as the *Lord of the Rings* trilogy enjoy the best of both worlds, with live-action shooting on locations that is later enhanced with computer-generated characters and digital image-processing technology.

Once upon a time, a day's filming had to be developed and then projected in a proper screening room. Now, a film-in-progress can be stored away in a laptop computer and viewed at one's convenience, as Fangmeier and Irons do here, with Fangmeier's children looking on.

"During my past career in visual effects, my function has been to create a lot of different worlds," Fangmeier noted. "I've worked on different kinds of films, some fantastical and some nature-based. I think my tendency is toward getting that realistic look. *Jurassic Park*, for example, was in essence a very natural film, not as artificial as others have been, because we [filmed] in tropical settings in Hawaii and put in our dinosaurs [to the live-action footage]. And then there was the *Perfect Storm, Twister*, and *Master and Commander*, where you don't necessarily see the visual effects—and that's what we attempted in *Eragon*. I've always worked with directors on creating fantasy elements that could not be photographed, and of course, this was the case with the dragon, which was CGI [computer-generated imagery]. But I limited [computer graphics work] to the dragon, rather than creating more of the world in the computer. Our approach was to build real sets and find real locations based in nature and take our actors there, rather than having them acting in front of a big bluescreen. It was very exciting to me to make everything as real as possible, to do as much as possible in front of the camera."

Director of photography Hugh Johnson checks light levels in Galbatorix's lair. The lighting scheme reflects the menacing atmosphere of the ruthless ruler's inner sanctum.

Peter MacDonald, a storied second unit director and photographer of action, was called in for the film's epic battle sequence.

"In today's event movies, where so much of it is visual effects, you have to walk that line of how to direct a scene with actors while understanding what the background is going to look like, understanding how something might play with a thirty-foot dragon in the same frame. And a lot of people are great with character stuff and smaller narrative, but they don't have that experience or that vision. Stefen has had that experience of sitting in a room at ILM and infusing real movies with visual effects that serve the narrative."
—Wyck Godfrey

Saphira, Eragon's dragon, appears in the final film as a totally computer-generated character. Flat cutouts and other visual cues substituted for the dragon's presence during the live-action filming, helping the actors to match the eyeline of the dragon that ILM would add in later. (Note, this cutout corresponds to the size of the fledgling dragon that grows into maturity throughout the film.) "Half the time we had Chris Newman, our first assistant director, saying Saphira's lines back to Ed," producer Wyck Godfrey recalled. "But we were lucky that Ed had a natural ability to play the emotion as if she were really there."

## THE PRODUCER

By February 2005, the production reached the next important stage in its evolution, as the studio called on the Davis Entertainment company to produce the film. While producer John Davis would be involved with *Eragon*, he was focused on several other films, leaving it to company president Wyck Godfrey to lead the day-to-day production effort. Godfrey recalls that when he arrived, some big questions had already been answered, from Fangmeier's hiring to staging principal photography in Europe. But there was a lot of pre-production work to be done. The script needed work, specific locations in Europe had to be selected, the full production team needed to be hired, and—perhaps most important of all—the film had to be cast.

Ed Speleers rides a dragon rig.

Behind-the-scenes shot of storyboard art for a sequence-in-progress. Note the monitor, complete with video feed from the live camera.

Godfrey already enjoyed a relationship with Twentieth Century Fox, having produced *I, Robot*, the 2004 adaptation of the classic science-fiction novel by Isaac Asimov, a book that had thrilled Godfrey as a sixteen-year-old.

Godfrey came to *Eragon* already familiar with the book. "I have three boys and I'm always in the children's section of a bookstore, and the book that was always prominent had a cover with a dragon on it—*Eragon*. I was taken with the mythology and the world the writer created. It was the kind of coming-of-age story that seemed like it would make a great movie."

A first-rate production team was assembled, including production designer Wolf Kroeger, whose responsibilities ranged from heading the art department that would design the world of Alagaësia in every particular to overseeing the construction of sets and environments that would bring that world to life. Industrial Light & Magic, as noted, would head up the visual effects work. Special effects, the physical side of illusion making, would be done by Nefzer U.K. and Nefzer Germany, which both drew from an international pool of experienced special-effects artists, including special-effects supervisor Gerd Feuchter and technical and crew coordinator Klaus Mielich.

Filming in the great outdoors has its benefits. Here, Irons and Speleers enjoy a break between takes.

In his first meetings with various department heads, Fangmeier discussed how to achieve the naturalistic look he envisioned. A key position in achieving that look was the director of photography (DP), responsible for not only camera work but also the lighting required for each scene. DP Hugh Johnson joined *Eragon* after meeting with Fangmeier in February 2005. The cinematography would focus on the lush green of forests and fields in nature, while the strategy for the camera work was to begin slow, with simple camera moves, and build along Eragon's journey until the arrival at the hollow volcanic cone of Farthen Dûr and the climactic battle, for which the full spectacle and fantasy would be indulged.

## MAKING *ERAGON* UNIQUE

A major concern of this pre-production period was that *Eragon* had to be unlike any other fantasy film or even historical period. The story, with its kingdom of rustic villages, dark forests, dragons, and magic, was steeped in medieval atmosphere, but Fangmeier didn't want the film to fall into the predictable category of a period adventure, opting instead for something timeless yet "modern."

"We wanted to have a contemporary edge, to not feel that you're in Ye Olde Town," Godfrey explained. "So we went for costumes that had a real style to them. Kym Barrett, our costume designer, has done the *Matrix* movies, *From Hell*, and Baz Luhrmann's *Romeo + Juliet*, so she has an extraordinary sense of style. When her costumes for *Eragon* come on-screen, you immediately feel like you're in this other world. There's even a technological edge because the fabrics have a sleek, cool look to them. That was part of this process as everyone brought their ideas to create this world."

"We worked hard at making *Eragon* unique. The world itself changes as the film evolves, from the normal to more fantastical at the end. I reduced the scope a bit, so there aren't too many distracting elements, such as too many action scenes. My interest was always to not let the spectacle overwhelm the story and the emotional involvement of the audience—I want people to be able to go on the journey with the characters."
—Stefen Fangmeier

**Brom and Eragon back on the road to adventure.**

CHAPTER THREE

*Casting Call*

*J*ust as the screenplay adaptation had to distill the heart and soul of the story, the actors had to embody the spirit of the characters. The casting strategy was to anchor the production with accomplished actors in the adult roles, with relative unknowns for the younger characters. The approach paid off handsomely, with a distinguished cast that gave the production "a legitimacy," in Godfrey's view. The veteran players included Jeremy Irons as Brom, the mysterious storyteller of Carvahall who becomes Eragon's mentor; John Malkovich as Galbatorix; Robert Carlyle as Durza; and Djimon Hounsou as Ajihad. The younger roles included British actress Sienna Guillory as Arya and Garrett Hedlund as Murtagh. "People perk up when you have a cast that includes John Malkovich, Jeremy Irons, and Djimon Hounsou," Godfrey concluded. "You also feel you have a chance to launch these great [younger] actors into the next level of their careers, because you have the safety factor of great actors in the adult roles."

# JOHN MALKOVICH
## KING GALBATORIX

**Actor's Résumé:** Starred as the manipulative Valmont in the 1988 period costume drama *Dangerous Liaisons*. As the would-be presidential assassin in *In the Line of Fire*, played a deadly game of cat and mouse with the Secret Service agent played by Clint Eastwood. Played himself in 1999's *Being John Malkovich*, for which he won the New York Film Critics Circle Award as Best Supporting Actor. Earned Best Supporting Actor Oscar nominations for *In the Line of Fire* and *Places in the Heart*.

**As GALBATORIX:** The former Dragon Rider who brought about the demise of the storied order now rules Alagaësia with an iron fist. The ruthless king will stop at nothing to capture or destroy Eragon and his dragon.

# JEREMY IRONS
## BROM

**Actor's Résumé:** The English-born actor's range includes providing voice talent for the villainous Scar in Disney's *The Lion King* and taking a Shakespearean turn as Antonio, who wagers a pound of his own flesh in a recent film version of *The Merchant of Venice*. In 1991, won a Best Actor Oscar as Claus von Bülow, the real-life aristocrat accused of the attempted murder of his wife in *Reversal of Fortune*.

**As BROM:** One of the last of the Dragon Riders, has been a disconsolate, broken man since the death of his own dragon. Has new hope as mentor to young Dragon Rider Eragon and once again proudly wields mighty Zar'roc, the dragon sword that Morzan, betrayer of the Dragon Riders, once used to slay Brom's own dragon—the sword Brom claimed and used to kill Morzan in revenge.

# ED SPELEERS
## ERAGON

**Actor's Résumé:** Born in Chichester, England, on December 21, 1987. During his secondary-school years, played the lead roles in school play productions of *Richard III* and *Hamlet*. Had never been in a film before but, on a lark, went to an audition for the lead role in *Eragon* and won it, beating out thousands of applicants.

**As ERAGON:** Discovers his true path as one of the fabled Dragon Riders. With his own dragon, Saphira, and Brom as his mentor, Eragon is determined to bring back the golden age of justice once known throughout the land—if he can survive the evil machinations of Galbatorix.

# ROBERT CARLYLE
## DURZA

**Actor's Résumé:** Played one of six unemployed steelworkers who form a male striptease act in *The Full Monty*, for which he won a Best Performance BAFTA (British Academy of Film and Television Arts) film award. Joined the pantheon of James Bond villains as the deadly Renard in *The World Is Not Enough*.

**As DURZA:** A Shade, a sorcerer possessed by demonic spirits, can only be killed through the heart. As one of Galbatorix's deadliest minions, the sorcerer is privy to palace intrigues (and possibly has schemes and dreams of power of his own).

# SIENNA GUILLORY
## ARYA

**Actor's Résumé:** The English-born actress played the legendary Helen in a 2003 television production of *Helen of Troy*. Along with Milla Jovovich, kicked butt in the science fiction–horror film *Resident Evil: Apocalypse*.

**As ARYA:** The guardian of the dragon egg, Arya is willing to die to protect the line of dragons. She joins Eragon and Saphira and the insurgent faction known as the Varden in a desperate stand against the forces of Galbatorix. Arya embodies both the ethereal beauty of nature and a warrior's ferocity.

# GARRETT HEDLUND
## MURTAGH

**Actor's Résumé:** Born in 1984, the young actor made his big-screen debut as Patroclus in the epic 2004 production *Troy*. His other film credits include *Friday Night Lights* and *Four Brothers*.

**As MURTAGH:** A young man with a past, Murtagh is the son of Morzan, who betrayed the Dragon Riders to Galbatorix. Desperate to expunge the guilt of his father's sin, he seeks redemption in battle.

"What attracted me to Murtagh is there's something about him that lies under the surface," Hedlund explained. "He's a character with secrets. He has the blood of the betrayer his father was, and when they get to [Farthen Dûr], he wants these people to trust him. He has this fascination with dragons, and when he sees the rumors are true, he's completely fascinated and wants to be involved."

# DJIMON HOUNSOU
## AJIHAD

**Actor's Résumé:** Hounsou's life is a rags-to-riches story, as a poor immigrant from Africa who became a star on the fashion runways of Paris. Breakthrough role as Cinque, the historical leader of a slave rebellion in Steven Spielberg's *Amistad*. Has starred in such epic productions as *Gladiator* and *The Four Feathers*. In 2004 was nominated for a Best Supporting Actor Oscar for *In America*.

**As AJIHAD:** A leader and general of the rebel Varden. The insurgents and outcasts bide their time to overthrow Galbatorix in their secret stronghold of Farthen Dûr, located in a volcanic crater in the Beor Mountains.

41

# JOSS STONE
## ANGELA

**Actor's Résumé:** Born in England, Joss Stone took the world by storm at fourteen when she won a British talent show for aspiring singers. She quickly went on to become an international music sensation. Has released two albums, *The Soul Sessions* and *Mind, Body & Soul*, and has been nominated for several Grammy Awards. *Eragon* is her acting debut on the silver screen.

**As ANGELA:** A witch who keeps company with a mysterious werecat. Eragon meets Angela along his journey, and she reads his fortune by casting dragon bones. In his future she sees many choices and great battles, along with grief, romance, and betrayal.

# THE SEARCH FOR ERAGON

For the role of Eragon, the production also made another of the decisions deemed necessary for translating the story to screen, aging the fifteen-year-old Eragon by two years. Wyck Godfrey felt a slightly older Eragon had broader appeal and an "inspirational effect" on twelve- to fifteen-year-olds. A talent search for Eragon covered most of the English-speaking world, with auditions held in Los Angeles, Toronto, Vancouver, Sydney, London, and other cities. But things were getting "down to the wire," Godfrey recalls, as the summer start date for filming was fast approaching and the production had yet to find their Eragon.

"We had to find the perfect kid," Godfrey observed. "The whole movie lives or dies in trying to capture the character you've read about in the book. It was the kind of role that needed to be embodied by someone who was a bit of an innocent, who didn't have a lot of experience in the world. We wanted someone who was a bit raw, who hadn't been in a lot of [movies] and could grow with the role. So the actor, coming into the role, would be going through the same thing as Eragon.

"I can usually tell whether an actor will work when I'm in the room with them," Godfrey added. "You're looking for the best actor you think audiences will hitch their emotional wagons to—at the end of the day, who does your heart go out to? The right person can jump out of a group, but there are also times when nobody is hopping through the clutter of the five hundred people you've seen. You have to sign *somebody*, so you [might narrow the choice] and pick from the six people you're looking at. Sometimes you think someone might work, but you're not ready to sign off on that decision. And then someone like Ed walks into the room."

Godfrey recalls that he, Fangmeier, and Priscilla John, the casting director from England, were at an audition in London when seventeen-year-old Edward Speleers walked in—and they all went "Whoa!" Speleers had performed in a few school plays but never in a movie. But he had that indefinable "it" quality the production had been searching for. The audition tape was sent to Los Angeles, the studio signed off on the choice, and the unknown Speleers was signed to play Eragon. "Everyone sort of fell in love with him," Godfrey concluded.

"Stefen was great—he put a lot of confidence in me, for a first-time director, to go to Fox and say, 'This is him, please,'" Speleers recalled. "He took on that chance with a lot of people."

## MENTORING ED SPELEERS

Speleers recalled how much inspiration he drew from Jeremy Irons, who had been as much a mentor to him as Brom was to Eragon. As with Eragon's own journey, Speleers had embarked into a wide, mysterious world, and his fellow cast members seemed to have protective feelings toward the eager youth, poised as he was on the uncertain brink of international stardom.

One of Brom's main duties as mentor is to make sure Eragon can handle weaponry. With Urgals and the Ra'zac chasing them on their journey to Farthen Dûr, Eragon will need every bit of martial knowledge he can muster.

The film crew lines up a shot as Brom prepares to give Eragon the day's martial lesson. "Brom is one of my favorite characters in the story," Paolini noted. "He's wise but gruff and loses his temper at times. But he genuinely cares for Eragon and does his best to make sure Eragon has the tools he needs to survive."

Eragon and Roran once playfully sparred at Garrow's farm. This sparring is serious—Eragon's life will depend on how quickly he responds to Brom's training. Soon wooden sticks will give way to swordplay.

The casting of Irons had been one of the production's coups. An Academy Award–winning actor with leading-man looks and a mellifluous timbre, Irons brought gravitas to his character. "The director, the producers, the general art direction—we're all moving in the same direction, and it might be different from what people have imagined [reading the book]," Irons noted. "But what can you do? I played Brom as I felt Brom was within me. Somebody else would probably have played it differently. But you have to make the character interesting and truthful for yourself and right for the story and hope you'll pull the audience along with you."

The pairing of the veteran actor with a cinematic neophyte was intentional. "It's nice to match up your casting choices with your character choices," Godfrey observed. "The choice of Jeremy Irons as Brom fit in with the journey of Eragon in the book. Just as Brom leads Eragon through the world of Alagaësia, Jeremy is a man who knows a lot about the world of movies and acting, and he's leading a young man into that world who doesn't know much about moviemaking."

Irons felt a special bond with the seventeen-year-old actor. "It was an absolute pleasure working with Ed Speleers, who's a bit younger than my younger son—he actually reminds me a lot of him. Ed has an enormous charm and intelligence and looks wonderful on camera—everything that you want an actor to be. He's a natural. The hardest thing is to work with a bad actor and try to bring a scene alive, but with Ed it's been an absolute pleasure."

Speleers laughed at the fond memory of their first meeting. "Mister Irons. Man, he's very, very cool. The first day I met him, I was popping on makeup and I kept asking, 'Okay, is Jeremy here?' And then he rolls up with his assistant. It was all very glamorous. He saw me and said, 'Ed, yeah?' I said yes, and he gave me a huge hug! That wasn't anything I expected. And all the way through he was giving me advice, making sure I was okay. He really nurtured me. I'm sure he was doing it out of his own heart, but at the same time, there was so much of Brom in him."

## THE VARDEN WARRIOR

Coming into the production, Djimon Hounsou was unfamiliar with the book, but he quickly grasped the essence of his character. "Ajihad, the commander of the Varden, is a true warrior," Hounsou said.

"You look at actors who have the strength and power to be able to do the fighting stuff but who also can carry a lot of weight as an actor," Godfrey said. "And we were huge fans of Djimon's work in such films as *Gladiator, Amistad,* and *In America,* where it's clear that this is an amazing actor who also has an incredible physical stature. Actually, that's sort of the way Ajihad is described in the book, so he was a natural choice."

Hounsou would appear toward the end of the film, when Eragon has finally reached the Varden stronghold of Farthen Dûr, which was dramatically staged inside a volcanic crater in Hungary. Hounsou's powerful, commanding presence was vital—a lesser performer would be swept away in the rush of events, because soon after Eragon's arrival, the Varden community must battle the forces of Galbatorix.

"The thing that attracted me to do this movie was the fantasy," Hounsou explained. "The sweetest part was coming to the crater set and seeing the exterior of the Varden [settlement], because it was stunning. It was so interesting, but also a little frightening because everything seemed to be going down, down. That scared me a bit at first, because it felt like

it would be so challenging to do all the fight scenes. But when it's time to shoot, you're trying to be in the moment and make it real and remember the choreography so that when you start, nobody hits you in the head. I like doing stunts, and I think it's the excitement, the adrenaline of trying to make it look good and real. And when you have stuntpeople who can take the hit, it's a pleasure. Take after take, the [stunt guys] would be saying, 'Go ahead, man, go for it. It's okay.' It's a joy to be shooting with people who are qualified and know what they're doing and are obviously excited about the work."

Djimon Hounsou was one of the veteran actors that young Ed Speleers bonded with during the production. Speleers recalled with delight his first real conversation with Hounsou, how a chance to chat over a cup of coffee at breakfast turned into a two-and-a-

> "That's the beauty of what we do—we're indulged and allowed to live as children still. We play the games that we played in the playground: There's a dragon over there—*quick*, get on your horse and gallop away! It's make-believe, child's play."
>
> —Sienna Guillory

half-hour visit. "We just talked about everything, like *everything*," Speleers said, still amazed such an accomplished actor would spend so much time with someone so new to the business. "In a completely different way than Jeremy did, he took me under his wing."

"You never really know if somebody's gotten anything out of you," Hounsou recalled. "When I've worked with great actors, it was only in later years that I realized how much I gained from them."

By July 2005, the production headed overseas for the start of filming. "For *Eragon*, you have to create a world untouched by modern man, where there are extreme mountain ranges and deep, dark woods," Godfrey explained. "You can't find that in the middle of California; you have to go out into the world and find it—Hungary and Slovakia became that place. The visual definition of what the world of Alagaësia was going to look like took on a bit of Eastern Europe."

The cast assembled for the main filming soon after. By then, the production had dreamed up and was building the world the actors would inhabit.

Swords of power, swords of good and evil. Zar'roc, Eragon's sword.

The sword of Galbatorix.

The cast included the various creatures from the land of Alagaësia. The tattooed Urgals are like mythical Stone Age men—violent and primitive. Once the enemies of the king, they now serve Galbatorix as his guards. Durza finds them helpful when he needs a little brute force to complement his sorcery.

Eragon has his fortune told by
the witch Angela.

# CHAPTER FOUR

# THE LAND OF ALAGAËSIA

The readers of Paolini's novel first encounter Palancar Valley as they follow Eragon out of the depths of the Spine. It's a long walk home after his failed hunting expedition, with only the strange blue stone to show for his trouble. Following a well-worn game trail, Eragon takes until evening to reach the ravine above the rumbling Anora River, which flows into Palancar Valley. By noontime of the third day, Eragon reaches the heights of Igualda Falls, the base of which marks the northernmost point of the valley. From above the thundering falls, the outlying farms are as big as Eragon's fingertip. In the distance, he can see tendrils of white smoke from the chimneys of Carvahall. Once he arrives at Carvahall, Eragon still has a ten-mile walk beyond the town before he sees the shingled roof and brick chimney of home, the farm of his uncle Garrow and cousin Roran.

Eragon faces mortal danger when King Galbatorix sends the Ra'zac to Carvahall to capture the dragon egg Durza failed to snatch from Arya (and which has now hatched). Eragon and Saphira flee Palancar Valley at the urging of village storyteller Brom, who accompanies them on the dangerous journey to the only place of refuge in Alagaësia, the Beor Mountains and the volcanic crater, caves, and ruins where dwarves dwell and rebels and outcasts have found sanctuary. Stops on the journey include Daret, a village set on an island in a lake (a departure from the book), and the dark city of Gil'ead, where the Shade Durza holds Arya prisoner.

The illusion of Alagaësia was created on soundstage and outdoor sets, at rugged locations, and in the computers of visual effects artists. The logistics of filming overseas were intense, requiring an international cast and crew of nearly five hundred. Producer Godfrey likened the production's organizational structure to a Christmas tree, with production heads at the top and descending branches representing different departments. The production headquarters for *Eragon* was in the historic city of Budapest during the principal photography period. This is when the main filming is accomplished, with the cast performing on sets and locations.

The map of Alagaësia in King Galbatorix's throne room.

From the start, the production stressed that the show have a unique look and not be derivative of any other fantasy film. DP Hugh Johnson recalls a meeting of producers and production heads in Budapest, where it was emphasized that everyone had to block out of their collective minds a certain popular fantasy epic. "We could not even *mention* the name of *Lord of the Rings*—we were forbidden by the heads of Fox. So we started to look at locations in Hungary, which was a huge contrast from New Zealand [where director Peter Jackson filmed *Rings*]."

By the time Johnson arrived, locations in Hungary (which included hilly terrain) had already been scouted. But other physical environments remained to be found. There were still potential locations to explore north of Hungary in Slovakia, a former Communist country with many steep, forested mountains. "We went to Slovakia three or four times, because every time we went there it was pouring rain or overcast," Johnson recalled. "But when the weather broke and the sun was shining, [the locations] were good."

Weather, as with any outdoor filming, was a major concern. Many expensive movie sets have been swamped by high tide or drowned in thundering rain, blown apart by typhoons or buried in snow. But Mother Nature seemed to look kindly upon *Eragon*, providing her own natural production design in the Slovakian wilderness. A location scout flyover to

one area arrived months after a tornado had blown through in one wild night, leveling miles of evergreen forest along a craggy mountain face. A third expedition to the same area arrived to see the encore, a fire that had swept through the fallen timber. The contrast between the grandeur of the looming cliffs and the natural devastation gave the location an "unworldly" quality, in Jeremy Irons's view. "It looked almost too bizarre to be true," Godfrey agreed. "So it became an interesting location for a darker part of the movie, Eragon's journey into Gil'ead. People will look at this movie and think we must have spent millions on this set. But in reality, nature did it."

## CONJURING ALAGAËSIA

The advance scouting work was of particular concern to production designer Wolf Kroeger, whose art department had to dream up the look of the world and fit it to the locations. "I'm always on the scout—part of my job is to find locations. Then you try to sell a location to the director, who has to approve it. Then the whole production and money thing kicks in:

Can we afford to come here? Can we get the whole crew here? What you do is start from where your production offices are and look within a circumference of ten to twenty miles. From there you go bigger and bigger."

Kroeger's art department formed a lot of branches of the production's Christmas tree structure, as he hired the heads of the construction department, the greens department, foremen, prop masters, set dressers, and painters. "I've used the same crews for years and I know what they can do," Kroeger said. "Good crews are very important, and I had an excellent crew on this one, all good people."

Wolf Kroeger was from the adventurous school of muscular moviemaking, where mountains would be moved, if needed, to achieve a grand illusion. "When I did the *Last of the Mohicans* for Michael Mann, we went up to a forest in North Carolina," Kroeger explained. "We arranged with a power company to cut down all the trees with [the proviso] that we would replant, which we did, and we had lumberjacks build the fortress from all those trees. I did *Reign of Fire,* a movie about dragons

**Production design of Durza's castle.**

The main house at Uncle Garrow's farm.

attacking London, and for that production, we went to Ireland and built a whole castle and the fiery ruins of London on a waterfront set for real, no CGI.

"The more you can do for real, the better," Kroeger declared. "I build things. I always build from scratch. [Stefen] surprised me, because he's a visual effects guy from ILM, but he said, 'I want as much real as possible.' Obviously, the dragon you do best with the computer, there's no question about it. Because of the computer, you can now do almost anything. But CGI does have a *look*. You have to be careful not to overdo it, or you know it's a computer-generated image and it becomes unbelievable."

Whether a film is made on a soundstage, shot in a far-flung location, or conjured on a computer, it's up to the production design to dream up the look of the world. Production design begins with conceptual artwork, and throughout a creative journey, concept paintings, drawings, and maquettes become more defined, until the dream is nailed down to the exacting specifications of architectural blueprints. Although many concept artists now use computer programs, Kroeger prefers the tactile quality of brush and pencil. His conceptual work includes big sketches, like panoramas, that stretch out six to eight feet in length. "I keep drawing and drawing, and if I draw it, I know every corner of that set."

"We've placed this fantasy in a world that seems familiar to us but is very imaginative. The beauty is we don't have to pay attention to historical elements such as what people might have worn in certain eras, which allowed our imagination to run free and have fun creating a world that will seem fresh."

—Stefen Fangmeier

Art department sketch of the waterfall that leads into the volcanic crater and the Varden stronghold. "A lot of designers don't do drawings anymore," production designer Wolf Kroeger notes of the increased use of the computer to create designs. "But I've always done big sketches. They can be six or eight feet long! I usually draw two or three at a time, so if I'm getting bored on one, I'll start another. I'll start drawing and explore."

When Wolf Kroeger first stepped onto the land that would become Carvahall, it was a field of mud in the Hungarian countryside with a bit of forest on the edge. The production design hewed to Paolini's original vision of simple dwellings built of logs, with wide porches and low roofs of thatch or shingle. There were no thin facades or fake materials used on the site, as Kroeger's philosophy was to work with real materials instead of indulging the time and expense of making something fake look real. The construction crew, headed by construction managers John Park and John Paterson, erected twenty stout buildings with solid foundations built of real wood logs, complete with thatched roofs. The greens department planted grass, trees, and fields of vegetables. As other sets were being prepared and the months went by, the crops and greenery grew and made the village appear as if it had been there for years.

In the film, Eragon meets a clairvoyant named Angela in Daret, who foretells the death and violence that will soon rage around him. (Christopher Paolini named the seer after his sister.) In a major departure from the city as presented in the novel, the production design saw Daret as a chance to create something totally different from the other

Art department sketch for Daret, a village on a lake.

locations—a city on a lake built on stilts. "The location for Daret was just an open lake in the middle of nowhere, but it was mysterious," Kroeger recalled. "It was fairly shallow, but we had to have a special dredger and pile drivers go in. Once the pilings were in, we could build on them. The city was like twenty to twenty-five buildings, some built on floating boats. It was a different look."

The final Daret set.

The Daret sequence included a ferocious battle as Galbatorix's Urgals attack Eragon and company on a bridge. The bridge collapses in the fight, which required the special-effects unit to use a specialized crane to ram underwater the poles that supported the whole bridge construction. "The hydraulic rams on top of the poles had to be working underwater as well, staying there for weeks after being implemented and tested," explained special-effects supervisor Gerd Feuchter. "They were operated with a special biodegradable hydraulic oil, as the lake was in an environmentally protected area. During the shooting of this sequence, we also had to produce massive clouds of smoke and fog over the lake's surface, so we used a special biodegradable fluid we found in France for our huge smoke generators, which we moved on large pontoons using several towing boats."

# FINDING FARTHEN DÛR

"The big set," as Kroeger called it, was the stronghold of the Varden, a spectacular setting inside a hollow volcano called Farthen Dûr, which included Tronjheim, the city of the dwarves. Tronjheim would not be replicated as Paolini described it in his book. Instead, it would be presented as the ruins of a once-glorious "white marble city." The scale was too spectacular to erect on a soundstage, so an appropriate physical environment had to be scouted. What was required was, essentially, "a hole in the ground," Kroeger noted, so the scouts began checking out rock quarries in Hungary, many of which wouldn't work, for various reasons.

Finally, the scouting expedition found an old crater that had been an abandoned rock quarry but was now a protected site. But it was more than that, Hugh Johnson remembers. "It was an old volcano. There was a plaque there that described how some kind of volcanic eruption had occurred millions of years ago. This was a vast area, with the base floor about the length of two [soccer] pitches and layered with terraces all the way up to the apex. That worked out really well since it's written in the script that the city is in a volcanic area."

The problem was that the location was in an isolated area nearly three hours by car from Budapest, far outside the preferable ten-to-twenty-mile logistical comfort zone from the production headquarters. "I knew this was the one," Kroeger recalled. "The place hadn't been used as a quarry for years and years—it was overgrown with grass. [The production heads] thought it was great but said no, it was too far from Budapest. I had to fight a little bit and say, hey, *this* is the place! I always fight like crazy for the images, if I believe it's worthwhile."

"It was in the middle of nowhere, but what made it serviceable was that forty-five miles away was a hot spring with a hotel," Wyck Godfrey recalled. "Hungarians love their hot springs, but it was off-season, so we could house our entire crew. If we didn't have that, we would have had to ask the people who lived in the small town [adjacent to the old quarry] if we could shack up in their houses!"

The crater was a case of being careful what one wished for. "It was another difficult location for us [the cinematography department],"

Production art for the Varden settlement.

**Art department sketch of the Varden refuge in Farthen Dûr.**

Johnson noted, "and for the art department, which had a huge job to build the sets and have them ready for us by the time we came around to shoot it."

As with all the design work, the art department's designs for Farthen Dûr ended up as architectural blueprints used by John Park and John Paterson's construction department. Blueprints for building on an outdoor location have to be even more precise than for a soundstage set, and especially for this volcanic crater, which had so many different heights and levels. Major post-production work would help achieve the fantastical scale, with footage of the set scanned into computers so that "set extensions" could expand the live-action photography in three-dimensional computer graphics. The design also had to consider Saphira, providing entrances and interior spaces big enough to account for a full-grown dragon in flight with full wingspan.

After the necessary permits were secured and a survey made of the site, many daunting tasks awaited before set construction could begin. Meanwhile, the clock was ticking—the battle of Farthen Dûr was last on

a shooting schedule that would extend into the autumn months, and film-ing at the volcanic crater set had to be completed before the onset of snowy weather.

Before Farthen Dûr could rise, roads had to be built into the location. "The first question after you find a place is how do you get the crew and equipment inside," said Kroeger. "We had to open up the side of the mountain and build roads going inside. We had to get a team [of moun-taineers] to go in and clear out all the loose rocks. Safety is a big number, always. This place was dangerous: it was slippery, there were different heights, it would get freezing cold. When it rained, water stayed inside because it was solid ground, so we had to pump the water out. It was quite an undertaking."

Once the building started, the set "grew in all directions, and we planted tons of bamboo and [other plants]," Kroeger recalled. The Varden stronghold was completed in three months. Meanwhile, Kroeger had been supervising different crews working simultaneously on exterior sets for Palancar Valley and Daret and other locations, as well as the soundstage sets that would stage the interior action.

The final set, filling the levels of the volcanic crater. The scale of the Varden settlement would be further expanded with computer graphics. "You're physically seeing only a fifth of what you're ultimately going to see," producer Wyck Godfrey noted. "[When making the movie] you have to have the vision to understand that and how the next stage of the process will be adding all those extra layers."

## THE SOUNDSTAGE

Unlike being outdoors, a soundstage allows filmmakers total control of their environment. A soundstage is, essentially, a big enclosed space—it can be as big as a warehouse or an airplane hangar—that sits empty until it is filled with whatever sets need to be built. The typical Hollywood soundstage is not only big enough to allow for massive sets to be constructed, but is designed to accommodate all manner of technical equipment, with an infrastructure that includes the "permanents," a gantry-like framework with catwalks up in the ceiling from which lights and even pieces of set can be hung. This was *not* the case with the stage at the old Mafilm Studios in Hungary, where the production filmed. Indeed, *Eragon* was one of the biggest productions ever to be filmed in Hungary, and although many in the production predicted a bright future for the country as a destination for filmmakers, they had to work with relatively primitive facilities. The studio soundstage itself was estimated by Hugh Johnson as pre–World War II.

"It was basically four walls—no infrastructure, no electricity except for the house lights, and even then they had to bring in generators," Johnson noted. "It was difficult for the art department and my lighting department to go in there and make it work. But in the end, it all worked. This is a country that's still coming out of the [Communist] suppression—it's starting to come out of its shell."

Thus did Alagaësia take form. The world that the art department had created would also influence the costumes of its inhabitants. A previous costume designer had been dismissed, so the production had scrambled to get a new designer. Most of the sets were built and filming was about to begin when costume designer Kym Barrett was practically thrown cold into the fantastical world of *Eragon*.

"I first start [production design] with sketches, but when the building of sets starts, that's the exciting part of a film to me. Day by day and week by week, you see all these different things, from the skeletons of buildings that become finished, the planting [of greenery] that happens on location, the set dressing. When the actual shooting starts, that's other people. But I actually have to create the atmosphere. To see it coming along, growing like a tree, is marvelous."

—Wolf Kroeger

The people of Daret, their costumes reflecting the nature of the floating city. "Throughout the movie, the costume design was dictated by the world inhabited by each tribe, their culture, and the way they live," Kym Barrett noted.

## COSTUME DESIGN

When Kym Barrett got the call to fill the void in *Eragon,* she had barely had a chance to read the script before she boarded a plane in Los Angeles and arrived in Budapest the night before filming began.

Barrett would recall with a chuckle that the work that had originally been planned for a couple of weeks on a few scenes and principal characters ended up lasting five months. "I had to redesign what had gone before. I had to take the flavor away and make like ten versions of that flavor and put it back in the world. It became, in a way, a very practical process. Actors I had never met would arrive at nine o'clock at night and were supposed to be working at six in the morning. So, overnight, I had to design something, make it, and have a few options ready. I had to do my best as quickly as possible, with whoever was coming up a couple scenes ahead."

Barrett recalls that Wyck Godfrey was a great help as she got started, as were other veteran production people who could share insights on the story and characters. But, ultimately, the saving grace was that Wolf Kroeger's art department had forged the path into the world, providing conceptual art to study and real sets to explore. Some of the sets, notably the volcanic realm of the Varden, were still under construction when Barrett arrived, but she could walk the paths of Carvahall and wander Uncle Garrow's farm.

"I went down to the art department and it fed me immediately," Barrett said. "Wolf is great—I think he is pretty much a genius. The village had all the animals, and different crops were growing out of the ground. There was lichen growing on the rooftops. You really felt that people had been there for years. It was otherworldly, but rooted in reality, which was amazing. Another wonderful aspect was all the unusual details Wolf designed—the roof spires and chimney stacks and gravestones. Outside of Eragon's uncle's house was a field of beautiful beehives woven out of buck twigs, which was so incredible-looking as a concept and told you so much about where you were and who these people were. For me, these little elements were symbolic of home and family and safety, of being surrounded by nature—and then [Eragon's] world is destroyed. It influenced my own vision, all these

69

**The costumes of Farthen Dûr.**

unspoken stories that support how you feel and how you imagine these people. The costume design doesn't come out of me thinking, 'Oh, black would be nice.' The only way to do this job is to ask, 'Where are we? Who are these people? What do they want and need?' The good thing was I don't think I could have walked in at any other moment and been visually fed in the same way, the right way, for me to do what I did. It was perfect timing."

For *Eragon,* Barrett needed a philosophic approach and a jazz musician's ability to improvise. The problem, and creative opportunity, was that, although it was "a completely formed world, in some ways it was falling apart," Barrett noted. Hundreds of performers needed to be costumed, and filming was starting with minimal costumes, samples, and prototype outfits, nothing really appropriate for shooting. The "unraveling" that had occurred in the costume department, Barrett noted, had a

As a bastion of the resistance movement against Galbatorix, Farthen Dûr has a more martial atmosphere than other places in the kingdom. These soldiers are attired like warriors out of the African kingdoms of old.

A refuge for opponents of Galbatorix's regime, Farthen Dûr has drawn peoples from throughout the kingdom. "For the costumes, I wanted to have the feeling of a cultural melting pot, like the old spice trade, where different towns and cultures flourished along the trade routes," Kym Barrett noted.

domino effect on other departments that needed to work with the final costumes, from stunt coordinators to visual effects.

Barrett quickly pulled together a core crew, which would grow as principal photography went on. She also drew upon local talent, including Hungarian seamstresses and leather workers. But Budapest was not like filmmaking centers in Los Angeles and London, places that catered to filmmakers. For one, there was a more hang-loose attitude among the local artists. An example was Oniko, a shoemaker who usually crafted only five or six exquisite pairs of shoes a year but produced forty pairs of shoes for *Eragon*. Barrett likened her shoes to beautiful sculptures and had offered to introduce her to contacts that might produce a line of her shoes, but the woman demurred—it was enough to make a few sublime creations and have a relaxing life of lunch and visits with friends.

There was a bigger problem—Barrett had arrived in July, a month when the fabric mills in Europe closed for summer holiday and shoemakers and wig makers and other artisans went on vacation. "Obviously, if I had started the movie, I would have ordered all my fabrics before they went on holiday. But what I would have done might not have been as good. I don't want my job to get to the point where you can get anything you want at any time, because then you get lazy. In some ways, I'm an impatient person, but I've learned to sit back and see what falls in front of me. Things always work out. You just work with what you've got and try to spin it into gold."

Barrett had materials shipped in from far-flung locations or begged local craftspeople to open their warehouses. Barrett also had friends and professional contacts around the world and, fortuitously, many were available when she needed them

In this stunning outfit, Caroline Chikezie reflects her regal status as the daughter of the great Varden general Ajihad.

most. There was Florice, a rock-and-roll pants maker in Los Angeles who had only a photograph and measurements to go on but provided twenty-five pairs of leather pants within a week. There wasn't enough time to express-mail the leather pants to Europe, so some friends acted as couriers and jumped on a plane to deliver the order personally. Barrett used a professional courier service to make four trips to India, bringing back suitcases of chain mail, while a courier from Turkey brought in shoes and boots, fabrics, and semiprecious stones to make jewelry.

Sometimes costumes had to be redesigned to suit the local talent, which Barrett saw as another chance to achieve something exciting and unexpected. A lot of decisions came down to what was available or could be obtained quickly. "I cut a lot of leather—that was one of the things accessible to me and cheap."

Eragon in full battle armor.

Barrett's costume department grew as the months went by. She estimated that by the end of filming, her department had grown to fifty or sixty people.

"If you can surround yourself with people who are really good at their job, and you know how to run a costume department in harmony and keep everyone fed and creatively engaged, you're kind of halfway there. There's also the political balance between the director and the studio, trying to keep the director's vision alive and supporting the DP and production designer, while understanding the restraints of budget and scheduling. You get really good at making fast decisions and delegating. You can't get too wed to particular things, or even that tomorrow is going to work out the way you want it. You learn to adapt. That's the realm I'm in."

—Kym Barrett

The world of *Eragon* and everything in it, from sets and costumes to props, had been prepared for the performers who would assume the mantle of their characters. "I was blown away by the house they created for me, where my character lives," Jeremy Irons recalled of Brom's home in Carvahall. "It was a wonderful set. It was fairly small, but was built into the side of a [hill]. It takes your breath away, the imagination of the designer and builders of these sets."

The actors also had to interact with something that was not there—Saphira, the great dragon who would be added much later, through computer animation. "In terms of working with something that's not there, it's actually quite liberating," said Sienna Guillory. "You can really use your imagination, and the dragon you see in your mind's eye is the most spectacular, beautiful, awesome creature you could ever imagine."

# CHAPTER FIVE

# Legends of Eragon

$\mathcal{P}$rincipal photography is generally shot "out of continuity," meaning a production does not begin with the first line and scene of a script and continue on to the final page—the last scene can be shot first and vice versa. Shooting schedules must work around any number of concerns, from weather and travel to the availability of actors and sets. Sometimes a director will desire a particular scene for the first day of filming to lay the foundation for the work ahead or to help crew and cast settle into the world that has been created for them. The most difficult sequences are often saved for last, as was the case on *Eragon* and the climactic battle in which Galbatorix's forces invade Farthen Dûr.

Cousins Eragon and Roran are as close as brothers—and just as competitive. Eragon's playful sparring duels with his cousin foreshadow the life-or-death combat he will soon experience.

# PRINCIPAL PHOTOGRAPHY BEGINS

The principal photography for *Eragon* began on a soundstage with an indoor scene at Uncle Garrow's farm of Eragon sparring with his cousin Roran (played by Chris Egan), a bit of roughhousing that foreshadowed the bloody combat Eragon would soon come to know. "It's always exciting to start filming on the first day, and we started with an interior fight scene between the two boys," Stefen Fangmeier said. "I think it was a great way to get the movie started, to get our young guys ready, with a bit of action. They did it all themselves, no [stunt performers] involved."

Each day's filming began with a meeting of all the department heads, with the "call sheet," which outlined the schedule, in hand. Chris Newman, the first assistant director, would go over the work and then the director would take over. As the director and actors rehearsed a scene, DP Johnson and his crew planned the camera work, taking particular note of the lighting considerations. After discussing things with the director, the grips and gaffers and the rest of the crew began setting up the lights, laying down camera tracks, or whatever the work demanded.

"We had English, Italians, and Hungarians on the [camera] crew—it was a big mix of nationalities. Amazingly, that worked really well. We'd start laying the cameras around, start lighting—it all happened. Everybody knows what to do and they all go and do it. There were language problems, but eventually everyone understands the language of film."

—Hugh Johnson

Brom locked in a death duel with a sinister Ra'zac.

The *Eragon* screenplay telescoped the book's opening chapters into a few tight, fast-paced scenes, beginning at Garrow's farmhouse and then cutting to the Shade Durza's ambush of Arya. It's night and everyone at the farm is asleep, except for Eragon, who picks up his hunting knife and yew bow to go hunt in the hills above the village. As Eragon slips into the moonlight, the screenplay describes him: "We get our first real look at him. A mop of hair. Intense eyes. No longer a boy, not yet a man."

In bringing Eragon to life, the director first shared his vision of the character with Ed Speleers, then left it to the young actor to find Eragon within himself. "Stefen would give me an idea and let me take that idea and play with it my own way. As the director, he has to take into consideration how the camera is going to work, how the audience needs to see it, how [the character] needed to perform. That's the time when he really said how things had to be, but he would let me do what I wanted with it. A book takes a long time to read, but I had to get Eragon [exactly right] in around two hours. So I had to be focused. I had to block the challenges out of my mind because now I *was* Eragon. That's what I had to believe.

And I did that, all the way through. My character grew so much, and I grew so much. But the main thing is I don't want people to see Ed Speleers. I want people to see Eragon."

By the end of the first week of filming, the schedule moved to the Hungarian countryside and exterior work at Uncle Garrow's farm. Key scenes included an emotional farewell as Roran leaves home and Eragon's astonishment as the blue "stone" hatches a blue baby dragon, which he keeps hidden in the hayloft of his uncle's barn and in a hut in the forest. The filming at the farm lasted for roughly two weeks before the production moved to the village of Carvahall, another set in the countryside about an hour's drive from the farm set.

"A lot of *Eragon* was filmed on exterior sets, which provided a challenge for us," the director

Cast and crew watching dailies.

explained. "Of course, there was the weather to deal with. For some scenes I wanted beautiful, sunny skies, and for others I wanted things to be cloudy and gloomy. And so we had to be quick on our feet."

At the start, the production generally found themselves working under balmy, almost springtime skies. But that changed, with lots of rain throughout the four months of principal photography. "It was a very wet shoot," Johnson recalled.

"We're always spoiled as actors because by the time we get to a location, the roads are there, the electricity is there. I think this was a very hard film for the electricians and riggers and gaffers. In some of the locations, you couldn't get a vehicle in, so all this heavy equipment, the big lights, had to be carried up or pulled up mountain paths. It was tough, but [the riggers and gaffers] are tough guys."

—Jeremy Irons

## FIGHTING THE WEATHER

The wet weather was also noted by special-effects supervisor Gerd Feuchter and technical and crew coordinator Klaus Mielich. The rain added to the challenges of a production that already had the inherent complexities of an international crew and the logistics involved in traveling to different locations. Once at a location, the rugged conditions often made it difficult simply to go back and forth between the set and "base camp," the central organizing place near a shooting location that includes production offices, trailers, and equipment.

"We had some heavy rain for two weeks beginning in August, which turned dust roads and walkways to puddles and mud, making it a challenge to arrive at base camp with the equipment trucks and became really adventurous if we had to get a boom or telescopic forklift to the

location," Feuchter noted. "Apart from the weather, it was already advanced logistics to get a huge international unit parked together near one location, as these were charming little spots identified as 'stone cave below ground,' 'small forest path,' or 'small mountain ridge.' These hard-to-access locations, so charming for

**Brom rescues Eragon from the conflagration at his uncle's farmhouse.**

their untouched look, had inherent problems. They were all ten to thirty minutes from base camp, and each and every bit of technical supply or machinery had to be carried to the set by four-wheeled quad-bike or entirely by hand."

As an example of the logistical challenges, Feuchter recalled two nights of shooting in a real forest clearing for the "burning-tree sequence," the dramatic ambush and battle between Durza and Arya. "The greens

**The drama of *Eragon* is set in motion when Arya teleports the dragon egg from the clutches of Durza. Here, the fateful confrontation between Arya and the Shade Durza is enhanced by the special-effects crew, who provide the illusion of a forest aflame.**

department planted already-cut trees to catch fire, and we positioned two large gas tanks in containers to have enough gas for the burn, put the gas pipes onto the trees, painted them, fireproofed the trees, and then the whole area was planted with shrubbery. We also needed telescopic fork-lifts, fire brigades, and gas refuel tank trucks on standby, in addition to the whole production's technical and unit supplies, catering, and actors' trail-ers near the location. This was two kilometers away from the nearest tar road and only accessible by a forest path."

The cast had some tough challenges of their own to face.

## ARYA, GUARDIAN OF THE DRAGON EGG

As with all the performers, Sienna Guillory immersed herself in the lore of Alagaësia and the backstory of her character, Arya. "The idea is that elves live for hundreds of years and are very much the guardians of the land," Guillory explained. "Arya represents the heritage of the egg and what it means to the people, the hope the egg has for everybody. Galbatorix has lived for so long that most of the country has forgotten where he came

**Costume design for the elf-warrior Arya. The ensemble emphasized both the fierce and feminine aspects of Arya's nature.**

**The final costume for Sienna Guillory.**

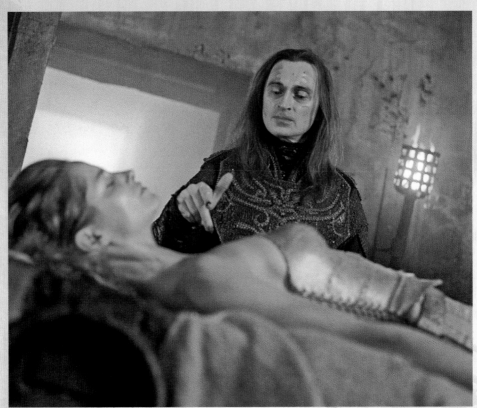

**Arya, a prisoner in Durza's lair.**

from, that he killed all the Dragon Riders and now wants complete power. So Arya's duty is to protect this last dragon egg."

Costume designer Kym Barrett helped the actress transform into Arya. It was an exciting experience for Guillory, who had spent years in the fashion industry and intuitively related to how costume design could bring out her character's inner qualities. "Kym and I had the same ideas about Arya. I think practically, and if Arya has been living in her clothes and riding with this egg for God knows how many weeks or months, she was not going to be spotless. So everything [about her outfit] is worn and soft, the handmade boots are spotted and speckled and aged. Kym is an extraordinary designer, the shapes and fabrics she uses, the exquisite way they move and fold."

Guillory's affinity for horses was one of the serendipitous discoveries that often happen on a production. "Sienna would hop on her horse and was galloping faster than half our stuntpeople," Godfrey recalled. "That's just one of those wonderful things when you cast somebody and you discover talents you didn't know they had that play perfectly to the movie."

"I love horses and have ridden them my whole life," Guillory explained. "For me, it's just as beautiful seeing a magnificent horse in a film as it is seeing a dragon. They had this horse for me, specifically for the rearing scenes, and they had sort of schooled him before I got on him."

The horse, however, was too wild and dangerous for the actress to ride—at least, that was what everyone else thought. "[The horse trainers] wouldn't let me get on him because he was supposed to be difficult. He had a marvelous brain and character but [at the beginning] was an absolute little pig to ride—everything you asked him to do, he'd do the opposite. And as soon as he did something you wanted him to do, he'd try to bolt off with you or buck you off afterward. And I just begged and begged to work with him because I thought he'd be great in all the scenes, even for the galloping, because he had this tremendous character. So I had four or five sessions where I changed his bit and saddle, I massaged his legs and hosed him with cold water. I worked and worked and got him to understand I wasn't going to hurt him or ask him to do anything he didn't want to do. And he turned out to be wonderful. And we had to do this shot with the helicopter and the horse guys were like, 'He's going to go mad, we should put a high gag on him and a big, heavy bit.' I said, 'Just let me ride him around for a bit and relax him and tell him it's fine.' And he was a kitten. I mean, he's such a show-off. A normal horse would see that helicopter and be like, 'Oh, what's that? It's going to eat me!' But he was cool as a cucumber."

"This movie is a fantasy, yes, but the fact that it's fantasy makes no difference. When you're making a movie, you're always making up a story anyway. Whether the story is set in the past, the present, or the future, you're surrounded by lights and film cameras and whatever. You are imagining a reality, and as an actor your job is to help create that reality."

—Jeremy Irons

## BROM'S STORY

In the movie, Brom is a malcontent who drinks away his evenings, railing against Galbatorix's tyranny. Brom's tipsy tales of dragons are taken as fairy tales by the townspeople, but Eragon, hiding a fledgling dragon of his own, is attracted to Brom's knowledge. Eragon learns, to his amazement, that Brom is one of the last of the Dragon Riders, but he

Brom, the Dragon Rider. "Just as children imagine a reality which is not real, that's what we as actors do," Jeremy Irons said.

Jeremy Irons glories in being in the saddle at full gallop.

also learns something even more astounding—that he himself is of that noble lineage and Saphira is his personal dragon. Brom, disconsolate since the death of his own dragon, takes Eragon under his wing to teach him the ways of a Dragon Rider. The instruction is conducted under stress as man, youth, and dragon flee Carvahall, chased by the forces of Galbatorix on their way to the Varden refuge.

Galbatorix would have many evil minions to do his bidding, from the ferocious Urgals to the Ra'zac, assassins who move at incredible speeds and jump unbelievable distances. But one of Galbatorix's most ruthless agents was the sorcerer Durza, who, as a Shade, could only be killed by a blow through the heart. "Robert [Carlyle] came in very much wanting to do a movie like this, and his approach to Durza was not to make the character obvious and over-the-top in his villainy," Godfrey noted. "You know Durza has an agenda, and with his red eyes and hair and pale skin, there are things apparent visually—you don't need to work so hard to force him to be evil. Playing Durza a bit more human and real makes him scarier, in a weird way."

## THE MAGIC OF VISUAL EFFECTS

Although post-production, the last stage of a movie after principal photography, is the designated period for visual effects, the process of conjuring the dragon in three-dimensional computer animation evolved throughout the production. In the new world of computer

Irons takes a break to discuss the finer points of swordplay.

graphics, effects artists work alongside the main production unit to take measurements on set, put up bluescreen where needed, and shoot "plates," the background photography into which the CG characters or elements will eventually be composited.

In charge of coordinating ILM's visual effects work was visual effects supervisor Samir Hoon. Hoon, whose ILM career began in 1996 as technical director for *Mission: Impossible,* had worked as a CG supervisor on the second and third *Star Wars* prequels. Hoon arrived in Hungary at the end of June 2005 and would not return to San Francisco until early December. He worked alongside the main production unit to plan for how computer-generated effects would be integrated into the live-action footage. With the assistance of an overseas crew, Hoon was even involved in shooting specific photography—the background plates—into which the subsequent CG dragon would be composited. The visual effects plates he had to shoot included extensive tiling (or pan and tile), by which overlapping photographic sections of an environment could later be reconstituted in the computer, allowing for more freedom of movement with the virtual camera. The visual effects filming included plenty of aerial shots for the dragon flying scenes, with helicopter pilot David Paris at the controls for the two weeks of shooting Hoon conducted in Hungary and Slovakia.

"We were always on the move—it was quite busy and fun," Hoon recalled. "We had an Austrian helicopter and we shot with a Wescam [an electronic and gyro-camera system inside a sphere] and a nose mount. When we had to shoot plates inside canyons and wooded areas, we opted for a small radio-controlled helicopter camera."

**The camera helicopter comes close to Brom for a flying-dragon point of view.**

Before Hoon had arrived in Hungary, ILM had designed the dragon's basic flight patterns through the art of pre-visualization, or pre-viz, whereby camera composition and elements could be rendered and developed in low-resolution computer graphics, much as drawn storyboards allowed filmmakers of old to plot out scenes. The pre-viz allowed Hoon to direct the helicopter photography to get thousands of frames of footage approximating the flying movements the director wanted. The flying footage would later be combined with the computer-generated dragon ILM was

creating back in San Francisco, along with footage of Ed Speleers taken during a London bluescreen stage shoot.

Hoon was joined in Budapest for two weeks in September by ILM animation director Glen McIntosh, who was already familiar with conjuring giant dragon-like creatures, including the ferocious fifty-foot-long Boga creature in *Revenge of the Sith*. It was McIntosh's responsibility to coordinate the team of ILM animators who would manipulate the CG dragon model and create the performances that would make that synthetic creation a believable character. "Samir and I would get back to the production offices in Budapest after a day's shooting and we'd start editing the cuts," McIntosh explained. "We'd edit to match [the point of view of the dragon] and for the continuity of camera work and lighting."

The helicopter work sometimes incorporated the actors on location. Jeremy Irons recalled that when a helicopter equipped with a movie camera swooped down for the point of view of the flying dragon, he simply transformed it in his mind's eye into the legendary creature. "Working with an imaginary character is easy enough. I did shots where Eragon was supposed to be riding the dragon and the helicopter was the dragon. There was a small radio-controlled helicopter with a camera on it and you knew the camera was the dragon's eyes, so you program that [into your mind] so that when you look at the helicopter, you see, in your actor's mind, the dragon's eyes. So in my head it wasn't a helicopter but a dragon with Eragon on it. Technically, it's not that hard to do because you've worked on it in rehearsal. Once you know where the eyes are, where the dragon is supposed to be moving and its posture, where its tail is, it's not hard."

A scene between Eragon and Saphira, after the dragon has been placed into the frame.

"I was lucky in the sense that I had [the dragon] from an egg. I could look at the egg—it had a color, size—and it gave me a way of thinking. I was able to picture Saphira in my mind through a weird combination of things, from images of dragons on book covers to how I imagined my dogs as puppies, how my mother would talk to me as a friend [just as the dragon] is supposed to talk to me. I used so many things. Having my own place to go in my imagination was actually more useful than when they sometimes stick a cardboard thing up or have someone talk back to me [to represent the dragon]."

—Ed Speleers

The creation of the dragon would take nearly a year and not be completed and integrated into the live-action until the end of post-production. "What was most important was that [Saphira] had to have a nobility, warmth, and ferocity," Godfrey noted. "That's what we had to capture in the look of the dragon."

**Eragon grows to love flying with Saphira.**

# CHAPTER SIX

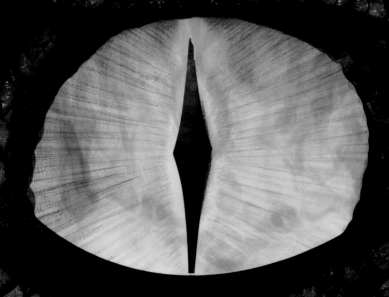

# The Dragon's Realm

$A$t the thumb tip of San Francisco juts the Presidio, a green and hilly expanse of land whose vantage point once made it the prize for strategic control of the western coastline of the New World. The longtime army base, which became part of the National Park Service in the 1990s, gained a high-profile tenant in 2005—filmmaker George Lucas. The $350 million Letterman Digital Arts Center, which includes ILM, is Lucas's state-of-the-art effort to shape the future of film into a purely digital medium.

Testament to the sweeping changes that had transformed Lucasfilm and filmmaking itself was the fountain outside the Digital Arts Center's main building, an Art Deco–ish base topped with the painted statue of a familiar wizened green figure in a robe gripping a gnarled staff— *Star Wars* Jedi master Yoda. In 1980, when Yoda first appeared in the *Empire Strikes Back,* Yoda was a physically animated puppet, but by *Attack of the Clones* in 2002, the Jedi knight was a completely computer-generated and animated character.

ILM had come a long way to its high-tech home in the Presidio. Lucas had formed the unit in the mid-1970s to create all the marvels he envisioned for *Star Wars*. They operated out of an industrial warehouse in Van Nuys, near Los Angeles, and those first young ILMers were as insurgent a group in Hollywood as the rebel forces who battled the Empire in the movie. They broke all the rules and made up a few new ones. They resurrected filmmaking tools abandoned by the industry (such as VistaVision film and cameras, a widescreen process introduced in the 1950s), took cameras built before most of them had even been born and bolted together new hybrid cameras, and developed the ability to program repeatable moves for cameras and models.

Arya and Eragon saddle up Saphira. The mock-up of the dragon's torso would be replaced in the post-production period by Industrial Light & Magic's computer-generated creation.

Today they are using advanced computer systems to push traditional effects to the limits—and they are still the gold standard in visual effects.

## THE DRAGON MYTH

Coming into *Eragon*, there was plenty of precedent for creating a dragon. The dragon myth itself has fired the human imagination throughout time and in many cultures. The classic winged, fire-breathing creature was described in the epic poem *Beowulf*, one of Paolini's sources when he was researching his novel. Beowulf, great hero of the Danes, slew a dragon that had been ravaging the countryside, but he was mortally wounded in the battle. So great was this feat, Beowulf's funeral pyre was built high and laden with helmets, war shields, and armor. The poem describes the creature's awesome power: "The dragon began to belch out flames and burn

Early conceptual artwork for Saphira.

bright homesteads; there was a hot glow that scared everyone, for the vile sky-winger would leave nothing alive in his wake."

"An interesting challenge was the design of the dragon," Stefen Fangmeier observed. "There have been a number of films that have featured dragons, so in some ways, we're dealing with people's expectations of what a dragon looks like. I went on the Internet and saw hundreds and hundreds of different pictures of dragons. But, to me, they all looked very reptilian. It was important to create a character we could relate to, so we could feel the bond Eragon has with her."

Examples of dragons in movies include Disney's animated *Sleeping Beauty,* in which the evil fairy Maleficent transforms into a fire-breathing dragon, and live-action films such as *Reign of Fire* in 2002 and ILM's own work in the 1981 release *Dragonslayer* and *Dragonheart*, a 1996 release

that took advantage of the emerging digital technology (with Sean Connery as the voice of the dragon Draco).

But 1996 was practically the digital Stone Age, given the exponential leaps computer technology makes annually. In recent years, the bar has been raised, including by Peter Jackson and his visual effects company, Weta Digital, which has produced such computer-generated characters as

Gollum in the *Lord of the Rings* movies and the giant gorilla of *King Kong*, which won the Academy Award for the best visual effects of 2005.

## THE ANIMATION OF SAPHIRA

Every production provides a fresh challenge, and Saphira would be unlike any dragon—indeed, any computer-generated character—that had ever been created. "*Dragonheart* was a really good attempt to make a dragon, but that character talked, his mouth moved," Hoon said. "Our dragon acts more like an animal but also 'talks' telepathically to Eragon, so we had to sell her expression and emotion whenever the dragon delivered dialogue in a voice-over. Saphira was not just a creature but a character, and she and Eragon had to connect. The most successful movie in which audiences felt a bond with a creature is really Peter Jackson's *King Kong*; they did an amazing job. But with *Kong* you have real gorillas to look at for the animation aspect of making it look real. Saphira is a dragon, which no one has ever seen, and she's also supposed to be blue. I don't know of any creature that big with that color; it's the smaller creatures that tend to have vibrant colors. There's a difference in what you see and what your mind accepts. You have a background that might be nice and warm, with moody lighting, and a blue dragon looks cool. It's always a challenge to fit that into the plate."

Early conceptual artwork for Saphira.

Glen McIntosh noted that he and his fellow animators were hard-core creature lovers, members of the unofficial fan club of renowned fantasy filmmaker and creature creator Ray Harryhausen, a pioneer of the art of stop-motion animation. In that process, a physical puppet is manipulated in increments, a single frame of film exposed for each movement. A second of film is made up of twenty-four frames—to get a second of stop-motion animation, that's twenty-four individual movements and clicks of the movie camera. Hand-drawn animation has the same challenge, only it's individual drawings per frame. A skilled animator's work—whether a puppet that's been manipulated or a cartoon drawing of a figure in motion—will have the illusion of life when a film is projected and all those frames run through the projector.

"Ray and George [Lucas] are the main reason so many of us are in this business," McIntosh reflected. "I'm lucky in that we all like big-creature movies, we all speak the same language. It's amazing to see a creature grow from a conceptual design, to make it look photorealistic and attach a performance, to see it composited and lit. To animate in computer graphics, we apply the same rules of animation that artists at Disney and everywhere else have been developing for a hundred years. It's just that in CG you're not dealing with a drawing, but essentially manipulating a puppet in three-dimensional space, to make a pose that can look good from any angle.

"It's been extremely helpful having Stefen as director," McIntosh added. "Not only because of his background and understanding of visual effects, but because he has supervised a lot of films that are very much based in our world, films like *Master and Commander*. I'm a big believer in looking at nature first. And the challenge for *Eragon* was making this dragon look real."

"Saphira is intelligent and has a sense of playfulness. She can be sarcastic, witty, fierce—she's certainly very dangerous when she chooses. As a character, she's so interesting and alive. When I was writing the book, I actually felt as if she were looking out at me, going, 'What do you want?'— which is kind of scary for an author, when your characters start looking back at you."
—Christopher Paolini

## BUILDING THE DRAGON MODEL

Saphira would go through the normal steps required to create any CG character. The dragon would be designed in a conceptual art phase, the modeling department would prepare the model that animators could use to create the performances the director desired, the scales and lighting would be added, and the final creation rendered and composited into the live-action footage. But for *Eragon*, animators were working out poses with a low-resolution version of the dragon even as the main model was still in development. "This isn't always the case, to work simultaneously," explained ILM model supervisor Ken Bryan, who headed a dozen-person crew responsible for constructing in the computer the dragon model that

ILM's animators would manipulate. Bryan had come onto *Eragon* in September 2005, after a conceptual artwork phase and a few modelers had been working on the dragon for a few months. "In a perfect world, you get the basic form first and then move forward with all the basic expressions. But this design was in flux and we needed to see her in motion, performing in some shots to see if the design we had was doing everything it was supposed to do. With Saphira we had to take a few steps back several times."

*Eragon* was a big production for Fox and, in addition to the vision of director Fangmeier, the studio was intimately involved in every step of the design and modeling process. As Wolf Kroeger noted, "I always fight like crazy for the images," and many in the production felt passionate about their conception of what a dragon should look like, particularly one likened to a shimmering jewel. "The biggest challenge was creating what our client thinks a dragon should look like, to take different ideas of a dragon and create something everyone could buy off on," Ken Bryan noted.

Although creature work usually begins with an artist sculpting and painting a maquette, providing a physical three-dimensional representation for a production to ponder, Saphira began with conceptual drawings from ILM's own art department and freelance artist Claudia Mullaly, a former ILMer hired by the director and the studio. Fox would ultimately approve a Mullaly colored-pencil sketch that pictured the dragon on her hind legs and that stressed the sleek, feminine qualities of the character. The 2-D image would have to be fleshed out into a three-dimensional form while also capturing the spirit of an image that was not a photorealistic interpretation but had a "storybook quality," Ken Bryan reflected.

"Overall, the studio fell in love with that picture, and that became the primary design focus," Bryan added. "We had to look at that picture and make it into a real creature. We had to take that stylized, softer version and make it real, with scales and skin and veins pulsing and light shining on it. It had to have that fantastic quality without becoming a big, creepy monster."

McIntosh, who had worked on conceptual artwork for Saphira with

Claudia Mullaly's colored-pencil sketch emphasized Saphira's sleek, feminine qualities, and eventually became the foundation from which the design evolved.

Jean Bolte and Carlos Huante, hailed Mullaly's work as "gorgeous." But as an animator, he saw challenges in animating a 3-D version of that approved image. For instance, the dragon was presented as a quadruped, but the front arms were shorter than the rear legs. "If she was walking on all fours, her butt would be in the air, which would not be elegant," McIntosh noted. "From a design standpoint, if we tried to animate that, it would cause problems."

There were also the inherent challenges in making a mythical creature believable. If the dragon could indeed rise up on her hind legs, those rear legs would have to be strong enough to support her body weight. Dragon wings also had no parallel in nature—unlike most winged creatures whose wings replace their arms and are driven by the integration of chest and back muscles, Saphira's wings grew out of her back and had to appear big and strong enough to help lift her into the air and keep her airborne.

## INSPIRATIONS IN NATURE

To help bring the dragon to life, ILM looked for correlations in nature. One animal that the effects house, director, and studio all agreed embodied the regal nature and physical presence of Saphira was a lion. "When Saphira is on the ground, we looked at lions, the rhythm of their walk cycles, how

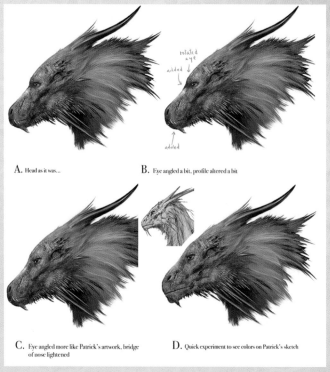

**A.** Head as it was...

**B.** Eye angled a bit, profile altered a bit

**C.** Eye angled more like Patrick's artwork, bridge of nose lightened

**D.** Quick experiment to see colors on Patrick's sketch

Saphira's face began to take on warm, mammalian qualities, her features reflecting the regal aspect of a lion's.

they bite into something or leap in the air, how much they emote in their faces," McIntosh said. "We looked at hours and hours of lion reference from National Geographic films and the Discovery Channel, seeing how the skin on their muzzle builds up, how their eyes widen when they get angry, how they look when docile or relaxed. So Saphira's face became more like a mammal—the jaw-joint connection is very far from a snake or crocodile, and she has skin covering the sides of her face. It was a fine balance, like taking a lizard with scales and assigning mammalian attributes in the facial area."

For the flying aspects, the animators saw a correlation in the flight of eagles. "A soaring eagle is regal and majestic," McIntosh added. "Eagles have a powerful wingspan, and when they flap it's not fast like a sparrow or pigeon. We actually wanted audiences to go, 'Wow, that's like a lion or eagle.' By its very design, we tried to create an anchor point for the audience."

With the approved concept art and design inspirations from nature, the modeling department began working out the three-dimensional dragon model. "Building in the computer is similar to sculpting in clay," Bryan explained. "There's a bit of setup first, where you model in polygons [the geometric shapes that are the building blocks of a 3-D digital model]

and wire frame. But as the [CG] sculpting work is done, what I see sitting inside my computer screen actually looks like a gray clay sculpture. But instead of using my fingers to push a surface, I use the mouse to select that surface in 3-D space and push and pull it. We did lots of tests and turntables, where you render a model and then rotate it in 3-D. It spins, like a lazy Susan in CG, so you can see it in all directions. For Saphira, we then began making adjustments to allow for a believable physiology while still maintaining the sense of design the studio fell in love with."

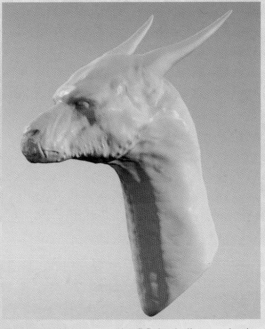

The modeling process in CG is similar to shaping clay. In this early phase before color and texturing, the image even resembles a sculpture.

# THE DRAGON EVOLVES

Since the look of a dragon was so subjective, almost every aspect of the creature's physique and physiology was open to debate. Ken Bryan recalls one creative battle in which he lobbied for a muscular hump on the back of Saphira's neck with a spine ridge down the back of it. The studio felt that looked too masculine, and Saphira ended up with a slimmer, more graceful look, adhering to the feminine and regal qualities of the character. But one of the points Bryan advocated for, and won, was for more muscle mass on the dragon's body. "At first, in keeping with the feminine look, Saphira's body was very sleek and smooth," Bryan recalled. "But I thought a creature as big as Saphira really needed some muscles. Even the anatomy of a horse, a mare, describes a certain musculature. So they let me bulk her up. [The studio] saw it and liked it and that got to stay."

The dragon's facial features evolve. Once the basic dragon form was decided on, the production began the fine-tuning stage—giving her expressiveness and personality.

The art of compromise often had to carry the day, particularly when the complexities of the technology ran up against deadline pressure. "We have to educate every client about [CG and deadlines]," Bryan noted, "and this show was no different in that regard. It's easy to review a CG model on a turntable and ask to make, say, the wings a little longer, not knowing how that change might impact many people. So as we designed Saphira and tried to get her into shots, we'd sometimes have to make the call [on a design request] and say, 'That would set us back a week.' And then we would compromise."

ILM ultimately produced a 3-D model based on Mullaly's artwork. The main problems were the short front arms and the length of Saphira's neck. "In Claudia's model, the design was good—until you got into the shots," McIntosh explained. "Once we got the dragon into the shots, we realized the neck was too long. In a two-shot, with Eragon on her back in the saddle, it was almost impossible to frame Eragon and not have the dragon's head out of frame."

Placing the **CG** model into actual shots presented many challenges. Since Eragon and Saphira have a telepathic connection, establishing an emotional bond between them visually was a top priority— but the team realized Saphira's long neck made it difficult to frame both her and Eragon together in a shot, and adjustments had to be made.

A major turning point was the decision on whether to "cheat the poses," as McIntosh put it, or bite the bullet and change the model. Ultimately, the production went for the change instead of the cheat. "Lengthening the front arms and shortening the neck was a departure from the concept drawing, but it made for a more proportioned dragon," McIntosh noted. "The ultimate design aim was to make a visually pleasing dragon that was consistent with the spirit of the character. Changing the model covered all the problems of how to get a pleasing composition and aesthetically set up our shots, which also served the story."

"Computer graphics imagery has been around long enough now that people assume, 'It's CG—it's easy!' But even though it's a computer, it's still the people in this process who have to do all the work. We don't have to get a hammer and chisel and go to a rock and bang out a sculpture, but the same level of skill and craftsmanship goes into taking these CG models and changing the sculpt. The tasks are the same—the tools have just changed. Some things are faster, some things still take time."

—Ken Bryan

By April 2006, when ILM headed to London for the bluescreen work for the flying dragon sequences, the modeling work had taken a good eight to ten months. But the basic model had finally been completed. "We've made great strides, gotten down to little baby steps, and now we're creeping up on our goal," Bryan recalled at the time.

## FINE-TUNING THE MODEL

With the basic form completed, the final stage was fine-tuning and finessing the expressions and personality traits the animators would need in order to create the performances the director desired. Of major concern were Saphira's eyes, which originally had a reptilian cast, very slanted and catlike and "cold," in Bryan's opinion. "Seeing her in shots, [the production and studio] realized it made her look like a scary monster—she didn't have that warmth. We spent weeks changing her pupils, making different brightness levels, making sure they didn't look like we just stuck human eyeballs in there. We clued the eyes into nature. The reason you know something is looking at you is through the eyes—it's one of the ways you know you're interacting with another being. We had to give her personality traits, things in the face and expressions around the eyes that would make her appealing. She had to look like a dragon, but she couldn't be all teeth and fire."

Weeks were spent making adjustments to Saphira's eyes, to achieve the right balance between a reptilian look and a more human look.

"The design evolved over the whole process of discovering Saphira through the color of her wings, the size of her head, the length of her neck," Samir Hoon added. "We see her come out of the egg—she starts off being ten inches high when standing. By the end of the film, she's fifteen

CG art of the baby dragon.

feet from the ground to the top of her head, her wingspan is thirty-five to forty feet, and her length is about thirty-two feet. There's not a lot of flapping of wings when Saphira takes off—she crouches down, using the power of her back legs and the thrust of her wings, so when she goes up, she can propel pretty fast. You have to study reality and then see how much you can bend reality to get what the director and the studio client's vision is."

The weight, the wingspan, and other physical considerations all fed into the way ILM's animators would move their dragon model through a scene, how fast it could traverse physical space. The animation would be aided by the Sim (for simulation), a process by which the computer

A later rendering of Saphira.

automatically does certain assigned tasks. ILM's Sim work, which was done by the creature-development team headed by Aaron Ferguson, used simulation on such aspects as the dragon's subtle muscle jiggle when in movement and the fluttering in the wing membrane when in flight. However, as with all things involving the computer, the parameters had to be set by human beings.

"Sim is a trial-and-error process," McIntosh noted. "Samir and I would view a Sim, and if it was too strong, we could tighten and dial in new parameters and run it again. For example, we made the flutter in the wing membrane more subtle, like the taut cloth on a hang glider, which was the example Stefen gave for what he wanted. But you needed to see those subtle little variables, things like the muscle jiggle, since audiences are used to seeing that on an animal. If that was removed from the equation, it would look wrong—audiences would pick up on that, even if they didn't know exactly what was missing."

# THE DRAGON COLOR SCHEME

A major challenge in the final stages of shading and rendering the CG image was integrating into the live-action footage the blue hue and gem-like iridescence of Saphira's scales. The final animated and composited dragon had to match the look the director of photography had created in principal photography. All movies have a certain look, a color palette that can be achieved through lens filters, lighting effects, and the photochemical process. The "color timing," by which the CG dragon elements would work within the overall color scheme, was tricky. In March 2006, Hoon got a color target to match to after he talked on the telephone with Stefen Fangmeier. The director wanted to shift the color timing for certain daylight sequences to "magic hour," that warm, golden light of dawn and dusk. With such targets in mind, ILM could then figure out their own color timing and color-balance their dragon with the live-action photography, the so-called background plates into which the digital artists had to seamlessly composite the CG dragon.

Saphira comes to life.

"Blue is a very sensitive color—you don't want to mess with or change those colors too much," Hoon explained. "So we worked with Stefen and the studio for targets as to what a sequence should look like so we could time our plates that way all across the sequence and get a uniform look. And they did the same on the live-action shots. Both the visual effects and live-action had to cut together, to have the same mood yet have it feel that a blue dragon was blended in there, irrespective of how warm the environment looked."

# SPECIAL-EFFECTS DRAGON WORK

The illusion of a flying, fire-breathing dragon was reinforced by the special-effects unit led by Gerd Feuchter and Klaus Mielich, which had to physically create everything needed to enhance and tie in with the digital animation. The evolution of Saphira had been of concern to the special-effects unit, as the physical effects for the dragon had to be measured by the stages of the dragon's growth from hatchling to maturity. Physical effects were important for what the production called "interactive dragon movements," particularly the sequences of Eragon flying with Saphira. "As we came closer to the motion rig shoot," Feuchter explained, "visual effects realized there were numerous shots that required pieces of action around the actors where the CG dragon would be inserted later, as well as specific moves of an actor that might be interacting with the dragon and which had to be shot on location. Our department was asked to provide quick, simple solutions for interactive movements such as dragon footsteps in the grass, when the dragon's tail might wag or slam against an actor, when the dragon becomes entangled in brambles, and gusts of wind as the dragon takes off and lands.

"Our credo is that the combination of physical effects and CG can work for an excellent shot," Feuchter added. "Use whatever you can get as a real effect, coming with all its physical presence, if it's an explosion, a [bullet] hit, or whatever else, and combine with the computerized images or elements where necessary. For example, in a scene where the dragon crashes, you want to see what happens when such a heavy creature hits the ground out of full flight. Visual effects gave us approximate sizes and distances, and we prepared the ground by digging in a thirty-foot-long track. Then we shot the wire-pull [a cable running underground yanked by a rig] along the track,

seeing all the grass, twigs, and leaves that were dressed over the track sinking in, which marked the track on which the dragon would be animated. There was another scene, when Saphira rips open the roof of Durza's castle and frees Eragon and Arya. The ripping of the roof was made in CGI. All of the broken and splintered beams falling down on Durza's guards with lots of dust and debris was a physical effect, created from breakaway beams, dust, and debris that was well coordinated and thrown into the set."

Ultimately, Eragon penetrates the stronghold of the Varden. The battle of Farthen Dûr, with Urgals and Galbatorix's elite army attacking the Varden, marked the end of Eragon's journey, the climax of the story, and the grand finale of the main shooting schedule.

Saphira greets Hrothgar.

# CHAPTER SEVEN

# THE BATTLE OF FARTHEN DÛR

The special-effects department helped Eragon reach the end of his quest, as young Murtagh leads the way through a waterfall that shields the passageway into the Varden refuge. Special effects was in charge of building the waterfall, which was produced as a thirty-five-foot-high and forty-foot-wide exterior set dressed out with dirt and vegetation at the studio. Underwater photography was required for shots of Eragon and Murtagh plunging through the waterfall, but the production was unable to secure a pool in Budapest that was deep enough to shoot underwater. Because of this, the exterior set had to be equipped to shoot the underwater sequences, which included a water-heating unit to make things comfortable for the actors. "We found an English and German company to provide a high-end filtration system to keep out bacteria and keep the water clear enough to enable underwater filming," Feuchter explained. "This wasn't a small task when working around a concrete basin with heated water, pumping up with all the oxygen that the waterfall brought in, next to hundreds of plants and soil built around the basin and waterfall set."

The old studio's electrical system proved a challenge for the pumping of the waterfall, which had to drive between 1,000 and 1,200 feet of water per second into the basin. "After our first tests worked out fine, the day before we started to shoot the sequence, each time we wanted to start up the pumps, one of the fuses

Eragon and Murtagh are confronted at the entrance to Farthen Dûr.

went, leaving our technicians more and more nervous," Feuchter recalled. "In the end, after changing some distribution boxes, it worked perfectly fine on the days needed. But the outdated electrical system of the studio had to be watched closely at all times."

For the Varden stronghold, Feuchter and Mielich recall that they had to prep a week later than scheduled, as some of the site construction was still ongoing, notably a paddy field within the crater that a subcontractor had not completed and which the special-effects team had to fill with water. The work for Farthen Dûr required the special-effects unit to "crew up" with more than forty technicians to create everything from campfires and settlement chimney smoke to Saphira setting the paddy fields on fire, along with explosions in a tunnel and collapsing walkways and towers.

## THE FARTHEN DÛR SET

In the *Eragon* screenplay, the Varden prepare for war by filling the fields and marshes inside the hollow volcano with tar to set them aflame and impede the enemy's advance. The blacksmiths' fires are stoked, and blades are pounded into shape and battle armor is made ready, including the massive pieces of armor a dozen blacksmiths prepare for Saphira. "[My] costume seemed four times my body weight—it was heavy!" said

Gary Lewis, who played Hrothgar, ruler of the dwarves, with a laugh. "Going in, I thought it would be dark and earthy, but it was astonishing to see these incredible colors and the embellishment of the armor."

Although "the Varden," as crew members nicknamed the environment of Farthen Dûr, would be expanded through computer graphics, the scale and complexity of the set and setting were still a marvel to the hundreds of cast and crew who would work within it for many weeks.

Eragon appraises his armor prior to the battle. "At the beginning, I had to go in for costume fittings and that was like going into a different world," Speleers recalled of his maiden voyage as a movie star. "But once you start acting, you're diving into water in a leather outfit or swinging a sword around and it becomes natural. It became how I expected it to be."

Hrothgar in the heat of battle.

"I've never done a film like this, but I have a nine-year-old son and this was a wonderful opportunity to be part of a big fantasy epic. I was able to bring my son out to the set and enjoy his reaction to it. The amazing thing about the Varden crater was not only the scope, but that there was a working community, a paddy field and windmills and smoke, energy sources, a place where different generations live. I had an idea of what it would look like having read the book, but it was just astonishing seeing this crater."
—Gary Lewis

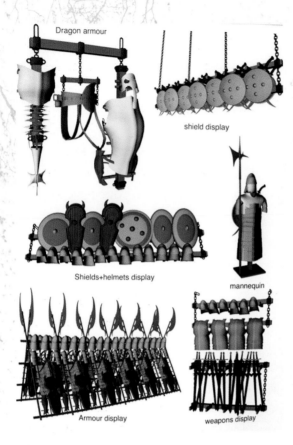

Dragon armour

shield display

Shields+helmets display

mannequin

Armour display

weapons display

# THE COSTUMES OF FARTHEN DÛR

"The Varden lived in this fortress city inside a volcano, so their world was subtropical, hot, a racial mix," observed costume designer Kym Barrett. "[The costume design] ended up being Afro-Caribbean, South American in a way. There were the elves, who live in the forest, and they made natural stuff, and they were allied with the dwarves, who mine precious metal and use metallic fiber and metalwork. It was very practical to each."

Barrett, as noted earlier, had joined the production on the eve of shooting and had to take care of imminent scenes on the shooting schedule. But she could anticipate and prepare for the final filming in Farthen Dûr and was ready by the time the *Eragon* production caravan arrived at the volcanic crater set. "We first worked on the high-end version of someone in the army," Barrett explained. "It was a cost concern, so the most expensive costume for a general dictated the costumes for the lower echelons, the foot soldiers in the main army."

Barrett's philosophy of turning adversity to advantage served her in Farthen Dûr. "For the big battle scenes, they didn't want armor that had been seen in other movies, but in a funny way, I had no time or money or people to make armor in the traditional way. I had to think of a whole

Eragon and Arya in front of Saphira's battle armor.

Eragon and Arya use their powers during the battle.

other concept of what armor would be like in this particular world. It strangely evolved, without expectations, because no one had time to have them! Great in that way. And our hero had to ride a dragon and fly and fight and be handsome and young and heroic—without lugging around twenty-five pounds of armor plate. I didn't want people to look like they were wearing big, clunky suits of armor, but to have it be more streamlined."

Leather had been the easiest and most inexpensive material to obtain, so Barrett used that for her armor. She called in Paddy Whittaker and Keir Malaen, couture leather makers from London. "Basically, we had to do body casts of all the actors and their heads and we molded leather to fit the contours of their bodies perfectly. Then we segmented it up, like jigsaw pieces, and sewed onto it segmented pieces of metal. [The result] was more of a flexible armor."

"For the fight scenes, it was mostly getting familiar with the choreography and the other fighters. You had to make it like a street fight, which is raw and organic, but also very clean for the camera, your [sword] cuts and moves. With the time period of this movie, you couldn't go into the fighting style you'd see in a *Matrix* movie or a Jackie Chan film."

—Djimon Hounsou

The forces arrayed against the Varden are formidable, ranging from the disciplined columns of the king's own elite army to a barbarian horde of Urgals.

# FIGHT TRAINING

Among the new characters introduced in the last section of the film was Murtagh, the young swashbuckler played by Garrett Hedlund, who is drawn to Eragon by rumors that one of the legendary Dragon Riders has appeared. But Murtagh is a figure of instant suspicion among the Varden because he carries the sword of Morzan, his father and the disgraced Dragon Rider who betrayed the other Dragon Riders to Galbatorix.

Murtagh faces off against the enemy forces.

Hedlund arrived in Budapest a month before filming to train for the fight scenes, which were led by fight coordinator C. C. Smiff. "I sort of got in the groove with training and riding horses. Every day for a month or two was sword and bow training and riding horses [for a couple of hours]. I liked the challenge of picking up a new weapon, learning your lines, and doing all this activity. It demanded a lot of concentration and focus."

"For the fights in this movie, we didn't want regular fights, like some of the medieval shoots with big swords," Jeremy Irons explained. "We wanted to get something between East and West. The fight boys designed these fights that required me to get used to weapons and the moves. But it was a pleasure—one of the things I love about playing characters is that you learn different things. We worked with very great professionals, and you piece together a fight sequence, you take it apart and learn it bit by bit."

For Speleers, the fight scenes were a reminder that he was living the dream Hollywood legends are made of. "I would get the call: 'Ed, we need to run through this fight scene.' So I would pick up a sword, sort of look at it, and go, 'Yeah, okay.' I didn't mind the sparring competition because right then I probably should have been [away at school] learning English and Shakespeare and falling asleep in class and throwing paper airplanes at teachers. Instead, I'm picking up this great sword and having someone teaching me these fancy moves."

In the movie, Brom and Eragon get their fill of murderous Urgals along their journey to the Varden refuge. Irons remembers the stunt extras playing the Urgals included actual huge sumo wrestlers. "They are very strong but controlled and wonderfully accurate, which is what you need because you're swinging things at each other and if you're a foot closer than you should be, somebody gets

Ed Speleers in the saddle of his Saphira mock-up, calmly awaiting the call to action.

something in the face. So you had to be careful. But those guys had been training for weeks, if not months, and they were long-suffering, patient, strong, and very good at what they did. They looked terrifying."

Ed Speleers recalled the extras playing the Urgals often grumbled as they got into costume, complaining about their makeup and the like. But when it was time to get in front of the camera, they were all business and became the fearsome figures of the story. "The extras just sold it," Speleers laughed. "They really got into it and would make primitive-man noises as they swung these big weapons above their heads. There were these huge sumo guys, and when you have people like that coming at you, it is kind of scary when the knives come down above your neck."

> "I remember when I had my first scene with armor on, I looked in the mirror and just took a deep breath. I could hardly move, could hardly breathe. But when the cameras were rolling, I got so into it, that this was armor that had been handed down [for generations]. You're just there."
> —Ed Speleers

## PREPARING FOR NIGHT FILMING

The big battle sequence at the end, originally planned for daytime, was changed halfway through principal photography. Hugh Johnson recalls that

120

the studio expressed concerns that there was already a lot of daytime photography and wanted a contrast for the battle sequence. "The producer approached me and asked, 'Hugh, how difficult would it be to light this for night?' This was a vast area with terraces, and it was very difficult to get any lights up there. But I said that yeah, we could do it. [My crew] thought I was crazy to even think it was okay. I spoke with my gaffers and key grips and asked if we could get any generators up there. So we did a helicopter scout to check if we could bring up generators and place lamps. The helicopters had to land on narrow terraces—it was quite difficult."

The preparations blocked out terraces above the crater floor that could be reached on foot and where they could place a camera. But Johnson's department had to go to elaborate lengths to rig the lights needed to film at night in the volcanic crater's vast, treacherous spaces. The rigging was accomplished with the help of a team of Russian mountaineers. "Some of the sides [of the crater] were impossible to get at, so these mountaineering guys roped out a lot of areas where we could undersling lights and put them on pulleys going right across, from one side to the other, so the guys could rig on the other side," Johnson explained. "They rigged it in such a

Second unit director Peter MacDonald in the thick of the action on the volcanic crater set.

way that we could take our lamps and power cables and all of that up there on descending rigs, like little trolleys. It was quite a feat, really. They had a huge job and we all made it work."

In addition to cameras up in the terraces, the camera crew laid down tracks on the crater floor while camera cranes would rise dramatically above the action. The filming would include Samir Hoon getting more flying Saphira views from a helicopter piloted by Mark Wolf, with an operator aboard controlling a Wescam.

The switch to a night shoot impacted the special-effects department. "After the decision was made to shoot the major battle at night, the sum of fires grew drastically," Feuchter noted. "The whole setup included large

Durza astride his steed during the battle.

Murtagh and Hrothgar anticipate the next wave of attackers. Garrett Hedlund came to the production ready for the battle scenes, having learned sword fighting for his role in *Troy*.

flambeaux inside the Varden, as well as hundreds of torches fixed to handrails and hundreds of torches handheld by the warriors, plus some thirty-foot-high columns of fire that we created, which looked quite organic."

It was late September when the main photography unit began its three-week shoot, after which the second unit film crew would take over and film at the crater set for another four or five weeks. The time of year posed an unexpected challenge for the hundreds of assembled cast and crew. "It was a good idea to shoot at night, but you didn't think about the cold—until you got out there," Johnson said. "It was that time when seasons change, and in Hungary things can change overnight. It was already starting to get cold."

The freezing night air was a harbinger of approaching winter, and the production had no time to lose. An early snow would be disastrous, given the Varden settlement was supposed to be inside a humid volcanic cone. All the pre-production preparations, the martial arts training, the filming that ranged all over Hungary and into Slovakia—everything had come down to the big battle scenes.

The camera gets the action as Arya moves in on an Urgal.

# THE WARRIOR ARYA

Sienna Guillory characterized the fighting style of the elf-warrior Arya as "Zen-like, very graceful. It was all about circular movement, and it's all kind of linked to nature."

Guillory remembers having to battle the icy weather as much as the hordes of Galbatorix, but she drew strength from the other performers. "It's such a tricky thing to keep the energy up, especially when you're doing night after night and it's freezing cold and you're wearing a skirt and you just want to go to bed with a cup of hot tea. And I had to run and [you think to yourself], 'Please, don't fall over.' But it was massively inspiring, doing all these shots where you've got a [camera] crane in the middle of a crater panning around and there's Djimon over there and there's Gary [Lewis] and there's like a thousand archers. You look at the other actors giving it their everything, and it really inspires you and you want to do the same for them. And it was wonderful having all these people here, the Varden people and the king's army. They're not all kinds of computer-generated imagery.

"Obviously, this is a big effects movie and there's a lot of downtime as they move things around and work out where the dragon might be and

**Arya slashes through a wave of Urgal warriors.**

Sienna Guillory performs a stunt.

what it is doing precisely. It's that whole 'hurry up and wait' scenario. But as soon as you get the call to action, you've got a million things going on, with people coming at you with sticks and weapons, and you have to save the dragon. It all just comes together, and it's the most exciting thing in the world."

## SHOOTING THE BATTLE

The crater set during the height of the battle, looking like something out of a nightmare painting by Hieronymus Bosch.

Each battle sequence was meticulously laid out. The second unit film crew was vital in covering all of the action. The main camera crew would shoot the featured actors and dialogue shots, and then, after "taking the action to a point," Johnson notes, the second unit moved in. The second unit was

led by veteran second unit director Peter MacDonald, who brought his talent for action filmmaking to the big battle. MacDonald's unit would usually finish up a sequence with stunt players substituting for the main actors. "Stuntpeople would take over the action from the actors, but the actors had been choreographed to do a lot of their own action, and they did it very well," Johnson observed.

The special-effects work included collapsing walkways and other structures, which were produced in Budapest as prefabricated breakaway elements and delivered to the set and assembled for specific shooting days. The dragon's flame that set the paddy fields on fire was shot second unit and created using a flamethrower device shooting a mixture of flammable liquids. A tunnel explosion blew out rocks and boulders, which were made of fiberglass and fired out of a tunnel mouth with gigantic air mortars.

"The explosion and collapse of the huge tower was one of the last major effects we shot at the Varden," Gerd Feuchter said. "It was prepared and shot with the assistance of a group of local blasting engineers using time-delayed detonators to give the single explosions and the collapse the best look possible. It could only be set up and shot as a one-taker. And it looked beautiful!"

The special-effects unit executes a one-take wonder, as they blow up one of the towers of Farthen Dûr.

After the main unit work was completed, the second unit shot in the crater for more than a month. It was the end of November, and after four months of filming, the schedule was finally down to the last shot—and then the first snowflakes began falling. Godfrey recalls it was either himself or Peter MacDonald who officially called the game.

Ajihad gets stuck as the camera moves in to capture the moment.

"It started to snow and someone said, 'Wrap, that's it, it's all over,'" Johnson recalled. "And then it came down—they got completely snowed out. But they had gotten everything they needed to have. The production was very lucky, let me tell you. Very lucky."

# CHAPTER EIGHT

# "That's How Legends Go"

ERAGON:
I barely recognize myself. . . .

ARYA:
You've come a long way, Eragon.

ERAGON:
They still doubt me. . . .

ARYA:
They will doubt you until you've proven them otherwise.

ERAGON:
And then?

ARYA:
Then they'll follow you wherever you want them to follow . . . believe anything you want them to believe. . . . That's how legends go.

—*dialogue prior to the battle of Farthen Dûr, from the Eragon screenplay*

After the battle of Farthen Dûr, Saphira and young Eragon meet to say farewell. Eragon feels an attraction to the beautiful Arya, while the elf-warrior notes the strangeness of fate, how the farm boy has become a hero and a legend has been born. Already, she tells Eragon, the Varden are sharing tales of his exploits in the great battle. But time moves quickly. Perhaps, Arya says, they will meet again—tomorrow.

"Then I'll be waiting . . . for tomorrow," Eragon says.

"Take care of him, Saphira," Arya says, as Eragon rises into the sky on the wings of his dragon.

But in his dark lair, King Galbatorix ponders the map of Alagaësia. Waiting in the shadows with him, a dragon stirs. . . .

# POST-PRODUCTION INTENSITY

By the end of March, with the Christmas season release less than nine months away, there was still much to be done for *Eragon*. Hugh Johnson was preparing to head back to Hungary to shoot a few pickup scenes, there were discussions about how to assign additional visual effects work, and the voice talent for Saphira had to be cast. "I'm filled with the anxiety of a job not finished," Godfrey noted at that time. "I've made movies where I've felt, 'Wow, I did it—the movie wrapped!' But in a movie like this, it's not really wrapped until the final print because you're doing so much in post-production. There are a lot more creative decisions to make that are *huge*."

Arya, bound for Ellesméra after the great battle. On the wings of Saphira, Eragon meets her on the road to say goodbye.

And as springtime blew into San Francisco on the winds of unseasonably wet weather, ILM prepared for its *Eragon* work to intensify. The ILM crew that had numbered twenty-five visual effects artists would ramp up to sixty or seventy people once the bluescreen work was completed and "the floodgate of shots came in," Samir Hoon said. Glen McIntosh's animation crew alone grew from nine animators to around sixteen at the height of summer. By then, there were 320 dragon shots in the works.

The visual effects work had begun in earnest in April, when Samir Hoon headed to London for six or seven weeks of bluescreen shooting at Pinewood Studios. The "flying work" featured Ed Speleers in three main

Eragon, dressed in the raiment of victory.

sequences, each representative of the growing bond between the boy and his dragon. The first, dubbed "the unhappy flight," had Saphira trying to fly Eragon to safety at his uncle's farm, with Eragon attempting to ride bareback in wet, miserable weather. By the time of "the happy flight," Saphira is bigger and wearing a saddle that Eragon sits upon as they finally begin feeling comfortable with each other. Finally, in the end battle, Eragon emerges as a true Dragon Rider, flying on and fighting alongside Saphira.

"I think this is the first film that really will show this element of flying on a dragon," Fangmeier noted. "It was a lot of fun to make the flying sequences very dynamic, like something we might dream about. Today, of course, we're used to being on airplanes. But, particularly given all the traveling I've had to do, I had to remind myself that it once was a completely unique experience for someone to actually be up in the air. I would look out airplane windows and think what a thrill it would be for somebody that young to be on such a powerful animal as a dragon and have that experience and, of course, to give the audience that ride."

With principal photography having wrapped and five months of editing complete, the production knew exactly how the visual effects shots of the dragon needed to work with the live-action and how the "flying unit" could shoot the bluescreen work with Ed Speleers. It was an efficient way to create the flying scenes and a major reason the studio pushed *Eragon* from a previously planned June theatrical release to December 15. "When we were shooting, we realized the only way to make the June date was to shoot that [bluescreen] stage work immediately after [principal photography] and it was going to be a mad rush to make that date," Wyck Godfrey explained. "In truth, the studio looked at both the release schedule and our production schedule and then decided to move *Eragon* to Christmas. There wasn't another movie of this sort coming out at Christmas and it was a very crowded summer. But all the *Lord of the Rings* films came out in winter, as did *Chronicles of Narnia*—Christmas was starting to become a place to put fantasy. So we said, 'Let's fill that position.'"

## FLYING ON THE MOTION RIG

The bluescreen shoot itself would give a workout to the M-rig ("motion control" rig). The technology, which allows for cameras, props, and rigs to be programmed for specific, repeatable motions and composite photography, had been around for years. But ILM was pushing its motion-control dragon rig, trying to get the most dynamic sensation possible. "The motion rig was driven by the dragon animation," Samir Hoon explained. "We had shot a plate during principal photography and we animated the dragon to that, so we had the position of where the saddle needed to be in 3-D space and tied that into the motion-control camera. The rig was stationary—it didn't actually move forward—so we had to tweak things, but the actor could feel all the movement of the dragon, the up and down and side motions. The goal was to get a performance that captured the sense of gravity and movement of the actor, all the nuances the M-rig gives you."

The M-rig was essentially the stuff of theme-park thrill rides. Speleers sat on a fiberglass mold in the proportions of the dragon's torso section. The M-rig work didn't worry about the head, neck, or wings, but simply the area where Speleers sat in the saddle. There were also iterations to account for the stages in Saphira's physical growth, defined as a ten-foot, twelve-foot, and fifteen-foot dragon, with foam used to build up its mass as the dragon grew. As the rig went through its programmed moves, the actor would react. If the dragon animation exceeded the limitations of the M-rig, the actor was directed to embellish his movements and energy— back in San Francisco, ILM would then make up the difference in the dragon's motion through digital animation. The bluescreen stage work made it as interactive as possible, with Speleers also reacting to being lashed by wind and rain machines, with the stage lighting ranging from lightning flashes to sunny when needed.

In addition to the Eragon and Saphira sequences, flying scenes included the demonic Ra'zac attack on Eragon and Brom, which had the evil characters jump on the back of Saphira, for which the live-action elements had been shot during principal photography in a forest outside Budapest.

"The animation drove the performance of the M-rig, and we did as much planning as possible to make the shoot go smoothly. After we got the M-rig data, we had the element of Ed reacting to the movement and we could refine and add details, like it's Ed on a living, breathing animal. The M-rig has been used on various projects, but with the level of complexity and dynamic movements the dragon had to have, we were taking this technology and really pushing it. We were attempting shots that had never been attempted with this technology, that I know of."

—Glen McIntosh

## COLOR TIMING

A major post-production concern, as noted earlier, was that ILM's dragon had to match the look of the main unit photography. Compositing the dragon into live-action backgrounds that had already been shot meant the CG creature had to blend in seamlessly, to look as if everything had been filmed with one camera. Key to the process was that the blue dragon also had to match the color scheme of the surrounding environment.

"In the real world, our skin color doesn't change when we step out into full sunlight or into shadow—what happens is the way light hits you affects what you look like," noted Michael DiComo, ILM's digital production supervisor on *Eragon*. "So even though our dragon is blue, if she's in front of firelight, she'll have a warmer tone. If Saphira always remained a neutral blue and wasn't affected by the surrounding lighting, she would pop out. It would look fake."

DiComo notes "color timing" is an historical term that refers to color values, and has nothing to do with measuring time. Color timing has two

**DP Hugh Johnson's crew lays the camera track, hurrying to catch the magic-hour glow of twilight. "We only had room for two cameras and it had to be natural lighting, but it was worth it—the vista was amazing," producer Wyck Godfrey recalled. "And then we had to shuttle all the equipment off and leave the two [actors] there to shoot big, wide helicopter shots of them standing there, alone."**

phases, he explains, beginning with the color timing of the background plate photography which, on *Eragon*, became ILM's guide for how they would color-balance Saphira to fit into the shots. In the first stage, checking for consistency of color was important—after all, a scene might be shot at different hours of the day, or a cloud passing in front of the sun might

**Sienna Guillory and Ed Speleers prepare for their scene atop the mountain.**

put a sunlit setting in shadow. But after scanning the film into the computer, the color levels could be manipulated to get the desired lighting look throughout, with ILM then able to match their CG dragon to the lights, tones, and contrasts of color established in the background photography.

In the next and final step, the film continues its journey as digital information. "Digital Intermediate, or DI, is the intermediate stage between us being done with a shot and before it's finally scanned back out to film," DiComo explained. "It's the last chance to manipulate color, to brighten or contrast things."

Samir Hoon took great pains to make sure Saphira matched the overall look of the film in the first stage, before things got to DI. "If we didn't color-balance the dragon, then when they went into DI and started to move colors around in the background, the colors on the dragon would shift dramatically and not look right," he explained. "We worked closely with the color timer to get a target for the look and feel that the director of photography was going for, so things wouldn't change dramatically in the final DI stage."

Although many filmmakers still prefer the photo lab process, most productions have been going into DI for the final color timing. Hugh Johnson notes the technology has been around for years in television, but he credits the Coen brothers' film *O Brother, Where Art Thou?*, released in 2000, as the first time the digital coloring technology was used from beginning to end. "That film started the whole ball rolling," Johnson said. "The facility to do this had been there, but people had never really jumped on it before that. Now we can change colors in a sequence at the touch of a button, really. You can control the color density, saturation—the whole spectrum of color. You can take light down, drop it off in an area. It's amazing what you can do."

After the final approvals, the digital files were scanned out to film for theatrical projection. Of course, the last barrier is to do *everything* digitally—the end of the medium of "film" itself.

"It *will* come, there's no question about that," Johnson says of all-digital motion pictures. "But, to me, digital is still a long way off. When you shoot a movie and see it projected on film, there's a completely different look. There's something romantic about film, more real. I find digital more hard-edged. It doesn't have the softness of film, and you can really see that in the skin tones of people's faces. But every year digital technology gets better and better. It's a whole different world now, these new tools. What's interesting is everything about making a movie is exactly the same—it's the technology that is changing."

# REFLECTIONS OF *ERAGON*

Ed Speleers, reflecting on the mountaintop.

By the Christmas season of 2006, *Eragon* was ready to be unveiled. "I think we were all very concerned to make sure this one is a success, and think about the [sequels] after," Jeremy Irons concluded. "For Ed, it's a big break, a big way to get into the industry, but it will really be a long haul to think about doing two others. It'll be very interesting to meet him if there's a second and third film and see how he's changed."

But whatever the future held, Ed Speleers observed that he made it through the production by focusing on becoming his character. "I just thought day by day about Eragon."

The spirit of Eragon was born within Christopher Paolini; he was the first to take the journey and be transformed. "The character of Eragon started as me—I think one of the easiest things for a fifteen-year-old to write about is him- or herself. However, as Eragon progressed in the story, he became very much his own person."

Paolini generally stayed out of the movie production, keeping his focus on finishing the *Inheritance* trilogy. He even missed visiting the sets in Hungary, swept up as he was in a European book tour for *Eldest*, the second book in the trilogy, published in August 2005. When he returned home to Montana, he plunged into writing the last book of the trilogy. (There is no set release date for the final volume of *Inheritance*. The book will be ready, Paolini says with a laugh, "as soon as I finish it.") "Since I came home from the book tour, things have returned to normal, with my family providing a comfortable working environment."

"I may end up returning to this world one day," Paolini said, reflecting on the upcoming completion of the *Inheritance* books. "But so many of these stories never end. *This* story ends with a trilogy. I've now written two books, and each time part of me thinks, 'Never again!' Writing is not easy. When you write a book, you expose a lot of yourself. But I'd rather be doing what I'm doing now than hand-selling copies of *Eragon* from the back of our minivan in the middle of a snowstorm while dressed in medieval costume. It doesn't get much better than to sit down, write your daydreams, and get paid for it. That's about the best job in the world."

And when the trilogy is completed . . . Christopher looks forward to writing one of the many stories he has outlined. But for now, he was content to spend his days living and working in the family home in that valley in the shadow of the Beartooth Mountains. "There's nothing like being at the top of the mountain and being able to see everything around you, for hundreds of miles," Paolini said.

❖ ❖ ❖

Of all the amazing sets and experiences, Ed Speleers's most memorable moment—the point where he felt the full impact of the sudden turn his life had taken—came atop a mountain in the wilderness of Slovakia. It was a setting that was the very definition of the "extreme mountain ranges and deep, dark woods" that Wyck Godfrey felt characterized Alagaësia, a mythic place they had to find as much as build. With its sweeping vistas, the peak was the perfect place for a scene planned for Eragon and Arya and worth all the trouble it took to get there.

For the flight to the mountaintop, Godfrey secured a Cold War–era Russian transport helicopter, a clattering, stripped-down flying machine with exposed metal upon which Speleers and Guillory sat, along with Hugh Johnson and a small crew and equipment. The plan was to first film atop the peak before sunset, then clear the equipment off the mountaintop and capture aerial views of Eragon and Arya. Johnson was after the warm, golden light of magic hour, which would shine on the peak and forest before the sun dipped below the horizon.

It was a thirty-minute flight to get to the mountaintop, and Speleers was in the thrall of both the adventure of moviemaking and the breathtaking scenery. The helicopter set down and the camera crew went to work "grabbing the moment," as Johnson put it, racing against the setting sun so that they could get airborne again before they lost the golden light. Guillory recalled it as "the most magical thing," standing on the mountaintop and looking out over what surely was the land of Alagaësia. "It really felt like being back in the time when forests ruled, as opposed to towns and cities," she said.

Finally, the actors were left alone in the magic hour, watching the sun set over the wilderness. "I was just so overwhelmed," Speleers recalled. "It was just Sienna and me, all alone in the middle of nowhere on the top of a mountain. I remember thinking I was the luckiest seventeen-year-old in the world. If I keep making movies, I don't think I'll ever have that same feeling."

# ACKNOWLEDGMENTS

My thanks to Michelle Frey, editor of the Inheritance trilogy, who contacted me as regards writing this "making of" book on the movie (and fond salutations to Wendy Loggia, who recommended me). A tip of the hat as well to Debbie Olshan, director of worldwide publishing at Fox, for supplying me with the materials and connections I needed to write this book.

The photographs in this book are the work of the talented photographers who documented the production. My appreciation to the still photography department at Fox, especially still photography director Steve Newman and still photography coordinator Laura Howe.

And here's a shout-out to Wyck Godfrey of Davis Entertainment, who was invaluable in helping to facilitate my interview requests (as was his assistant Elek Hendrickson, in handling my calls). On the ILM side, I have Barbara Bellanca to thank for helping me get the visual effects perspective.

A slow bow of respect to all the talented people who shared their thoughts with me, especially to Christopher Paolini, who is an inspiration—Chris, may the sun always illuminate your path ahead and may the wind always be at your back.

A personal word of thanks and love to my mother, who proofreads my manuscripts (and while I'm at it, love and hugs to my father and brothers and sisters: Katherine, Maria, Patrick, Peter, and Teresa).

Finally, my appreciation and admiration to my literary agent, John Silbersack, who wrapped everything up like a Christmas present.

—M.C.V.

# NOTES

My thanks to Debbie Olshan at Fox for providing me with transcripts of the electronic press kit, from which this book derived quotes from the director and actors (with their comments edited for editorial and continuity concerns).

All other interviews were conducted by this writer. Special-effects supervisor Gerd Feuchter and special-effects technical and crew coordinator Klaus Mielich together answered my questions via an e-mail document from Europe. The quotes ascribed to Feuchter and references to the special-effects work were taken from this document.

In addition to this material, outside reference works were occasionally consulted, and their citations are below.

## CHAPTER ONE: THE DREAMING

The she-wolf story was taken from "The Call of the Wild," one of the stories "edited, told, and retold" by Richard Erdoes in *Tales from the American Frontier*, a title in the Pantheon Fairy Tale and Folklore Library (New York: Pantheon Books, 1991), pp. 365–369.

## CHAPTER SIX: THE DRAGON'S REALM

The background history on Industrial Light & Magic from the author's *Industrial Light + Magic: Into the Digital Realm* (New York: Del Rey, 1996), pp. 6–7. (This book was also referenced for background on the ILM career of Stefen Fangmeier.)

Dragon description from *Beowulf* from Seamus Heaney, *Beowulf: A New Verse Translation* (New York: Farrar, Straus and Giroux, 2000), p. 157.

## CHAPTER EIGHT: "THAT'S HOW LEGENDS GO"

Quote from screenplay that opens the chapter from Fox 2000 Pictures, *Eragon* screenplay by Peter Buchman, copy inclusive of all revisions through "Double Green Revisions" of October 24, 2005; with previous revisions by Lawrence Konner & Mark Rosenthal & Jesse Wigutow; current revisions by Jesse Wigutow. Copyright © 2005, Twentieth Century Fox Film Corporation.

## ABOUT THE AUTHOR

**Mark Cotta Vaz** is the author of twenty-one books, including four *New York Times* bestsellers. His works include the award-winning *The Invisible Art: The Legends of Movie Matte Painting* (co-authored with filmmaker Craig Barron), which won the Theatre Library Association Award in 2002 and the United States Institute for Theatre Technology's Golden Pen Award in 2004. His recent biographical work, *Living Dangerously: The Adventures of Merian C. Cooper, Creator of KING KONG,* made the *Los Angeles Times* bestseller list.